inside

makers: fashion

Marcia Sherrill
Carey Adina Karmel

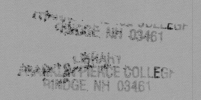
THE MONACELLI PRESS

Contents

Gurus

Players

First published in the United
States of America in 2002 by
The Monacelli Press, Inc.
10 East 92nd Street
New York, New York 10128.

Library of Congress Control Number:
2002102552
ISBN: 1-58093-099-9

Printed and bound in Italy

Project coordinators: Cissy Sullivan,
Natalie Martin Schettini, and
Camille Smith
Editor: Andrea E. Monfried
Designer: Pentagram/Esther Bridavsky
and Michael Bierut
Photo contributors: Timothy Greenfield-
Sanders, Anna Clopet

Acknowledgments

The daunting scope of this book would have been unthinkable without the careful coordination of Cissy Sullivan, Natalie Martin Schettini, and Camille Smith.

We owe much to all of our helpful and faithful friends and colleagues, especially Hilary Lewis, Sarah Jane Freymann, Edward Smith, Eli Vigliano, Sandy Thurman, Ron Saleh, Shepard Saltzman, Justin Milrad, Marcia Stevens, Jeanette Warner-Goldstein, Kim Zimmerman, Marianne Townsend, Rafael Guerra, Laura Fisher-Kaiser, Nora Feller, Kathyrn Dianos, and Diane and Toby Jenkins.

For their hospitality and help in Paris, we thank Marianne and Alex Karmel and Elena Ruth Sassower. For proofreading the text in several stages, we are grateful to Michele Falkow and Carol Deegan.

This book is dedicated to devoted families everywhere, and especially to our supportive husbands, Pepe Karmel and William Kleinberg, and to future stylemakers Remy Karmel, Caleb Karmel, and Anabelle Sherrill Kleinberg.

Finally, we give thanks to our stylish and loving mothers, Doris Lipson Sassower and Mary Jo Sherrill, and to our fathers, George Sassower and Jerry Sherrill.

Preface

TAKE CARE OF THE LUXURIES, Oscar Wilde said, and the necessities will take care of themselves. Perhaps all we need are food and shelter. But what we really *want* are clothes, shoes, and handbags. And we know you, the reader of this book, agree. There are millions of us obsessed with style. And that brings us to the question behind *Stylemakers:* who designs the styles the world wears?

The obvious answer: designers. At least that's the impression that comes from fashion magazines and daily papers. High-strung or laid-back, elegant or grungy, poetic or inarticulate, designers capture the public imagination. And since we ourselves are designers, we might consider leaving it at that.

But if we have learned anything from our experience in the fashion world, it is how many *other* hard-working, talented, insightful people it takes to create the styles people love—and hate. Sometimes friends outside the fashion world would ask us: "Why is everything puce this year?" "Why are skirts so tight?" "Why are heels so high?" We would answer, "Oh, they decided that a couple of years ago." "Who are *they?*" asked our friends.

This book is intended to answer that question. As we thought over all the people who play critical roles in the fashion industry but are *not* designers, we found three distinct groups. There are "prophets," who predict (or determine) fashion trends years in advance. There are "gurus," who survey the enormous range of clothes and accessories produced each year and intuit a small number of trends and styles worth celebrating and promoting. And there are "players," the businessmen and -women who place their hard work and organizational skills at the service of someone else's imagination.

Some of these people we knew from our own experiences as designers. Others we knew only by reputation. Still others we located through the fashion grapevine. The more than eighty remarkable people in this book do not constitute a comprehensive survey of the *éminences grises* behind the multicolored facade of the fashion world, but we think they provide a representative sample. By the time this book is published, some of them will have changed employers and job titles. But they will continue to play a critical role in determining clothes and accessories to admire, buy, wear.

Whether you, our reader, are an aspiring designer, fashion plate, or intrigued observer of the kaleidoscope of style, we hope this book will help you understand the *real* life of the fashion world, and the dedicated stylemakers who keep it in motion.

Pro

Prophets

Long before a garment is conceived by a designer or a textile pattern drawn by a fabric designer, a corps of adventurers searches the world over for the next idea. Theirs is a never-ending quest for the emerging style trends that inspire the design community. These futurists or "cool hunters" stalk the next movement in New York's trendy Nolita, Milan's canal district, and London's West End— the incubators of tomorrow's cutting-edge looks. Grunge, punk, techno-rock, the rise of body art, the hip-hop invasion: such trends have permeated every level of fashion and lifestyle.

Designers have their own ideas, but many of these loom large in the social unconscious well before they are transformed from inchoate feeling into fashion rendering. The nascent whisperings of a new street style need authoring—words and images to compel them forward. The trend forecasters and color gurus start their work as much as two years before a fashion season. Their intuition and color predictions influence the fabrics and trims, the silhouettes and textures, that beget the sketch, then the sample, and finally the garment.

The trend prognosticators who prophesy fashion's futures are hardly isolated, head-in-the-cloud ascetics. On the contrary, they use their special instincts to spawn businesses that employ dozens of style editors. The trend presentations given at least twice a year by fashion's seers are essential to designers, since each lifestyle trend dictates its own colors, motifs, and fabric directions. At these lectures hundreds of designers and product developers sit mesmerized.

At the giant textile shows—as much as a year before the fashion season in question—designers traverse the aisles armed with their amassed information and begin an arduous process of editing. But it is the rare designer who takes to the aisles alone. Many are accompanied by a muse, a person whose instinctive taste inspires that of the designer. The muse may guide the designer's hand and eye to a particular fabric or trimming or even restaurant interior. Friend to the designer's ego, ennobler or embodiment of a specific idea, model in the atelier, the muse plays a pivotal role.

Others creating the looks of the labels are the visual messengers: the magazine editors and graphic designers who not only tease new meaning out of clothing but continually propel fashion forward. Whether in illustration, layout, or museum show, the graphics of fashion are as telling as any other characteristic.

The fashion world has its own cadre of celebrants. Garbed in the newest new thing, they embody the pages of avant-garde magazines, seeming almost like a costume show escaped from its vitrine. These extremists operate at the industry's edge, ushering in the most exuberant aspect of every season's trends. Along the party and runway circuit that is the fashion world, these visionaries affect the media that will in turn influence the entire industry. Perhaps they are the truest prophets of fashion as the word derives from the Greek: "to speak for the gods," to lead a cause.

The Futurists: Forecasting the Trends

Why do designers appear to share so many ideas? Why does red suddenly appear in every store window? Why do a dozen collections from Milan to New York feature an asymmetrical handkerchief hemline? While most designers lay claim to their looks as original, in fact each silhouette, fabric choice, and color selection starts far away from the designer's studio or sketch pad. New fashion trends are actually channeled to the design community by professional trend and color forecasters.

When trend oracle Li Edelkoort comes from Paris to lecture at New York's Fashion Institute of Technology, designers rush from the auditorium to their workrooms and quickly revise their sketches to incorporate her ideas about future trends. Forecasters like Haysun Hahn, David Wolfe, and Sebastien de Diesbach work mainly in abstract concepts, using keywords like "comfort" and "bohemian" to guide the designer's hand. But these crystal-ball gazers also give specific trend data on everything from jacket length to pocket detail to heel height.

A blown-glass ornament suspended from a wire, a rustic Mexican table-cloth, industrial felt pillows, wheat in vases—all surround the throne of uber–trend forecaster Li Edelkoort. Trays upon trays of slides fill the offices of her company, Trend Union, which is located in the industrial out-skirts of Paris. Edelkoort is a prophet for several industries, fashion chief among them. She enters the room wearing an ethereal but humble cloth garment, a creation from her team's new line of world indigenous crafts. The talents of this demi-goddess of

the essential story." Edelkoort's eye-catching arrays allowed designers to make sense of the endless sea of fab-rics at row after row of textile booths.

Edelkoort has been forecasting for thirty years; she is nearly messianic as she proselytizes at her packed biannual lectures in New York and Paris. She is consistently on target in her trend predictions. The books, magazines, and design dossiers she publishes for her roster of big-name manufacturing and retail clients have transformed the global

absorb this information. They will go for a detail or a style but they don't know why." Edelkoort does know why, and explaining why is a big part of her job.

As she rifles through Trend Union's magnificently produced trend inspi-ration books, Edelkoort stresses that the gist of her job is strategy and brand positioning. With the once staid shoe company Camper, she says, "When fashion hit shoes they felt they had to become more fash-ionable; we told them no, it will come around, it will return to earth. Stay close to your roots." Their success proves her point. Camper shoe sales have risen sharply, and they neither alienated their core customers nor lost the youthful urban buyer. Edelkoort saved them from a costly repositioning of the brand, claiming, "I like the power of making a better thing, and to do this you have to be focused—we do not encourage change simply for change's sake."

"Fashion is driven now much more by the way we want to live."

trend were first spotted in art school in her native Holland. Then, as a fashion coordinator for a Dutch department store, she says, "I was exposed to color cards, seasonal trends, and how to define a trend. How would you give it a name? How would you show it to personnel? How would you show it to the press?" Her visionary work for the French textile exposition Premiere Vision landed her on the world map: "We put the fabrics into displays in a way that enabled the buyers to grasp

aesthetic. Edelkoort and her thirty-five-member staff give clients a coherent message and a defining intuition that lay the groundwork for color prediction, textile design, and clothing creation. She sees tremen-dous change resulting from the explosion of information and the concomitant technology: "Fashion is driven now much more by the way we want to live; it is much more related to other categories. People are better informed but they don't necessarily know how to

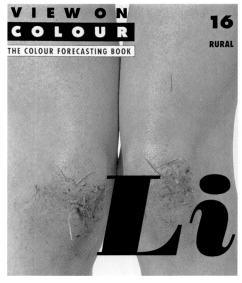

VIEW ON COLOUR

THE COLOUR FORECASTING BOOK

16

RURAL

Li

Timothy Greenfield-Sanders

Edelkoort
Fashion's Foremost Soothsayer

bloom

a horti-cultural view

The Heart of the Matter

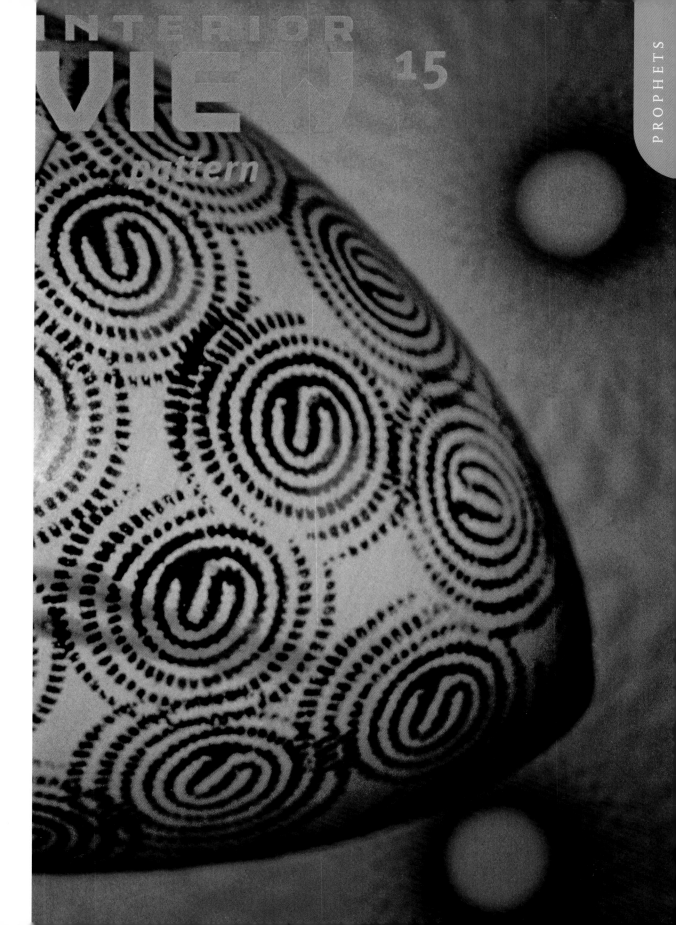

INTERIOR
VIEW
pattern

15

Haysun

"I'm probably a better communicator— and my antennae may be a bit higher."

Oracle for
Global Companies

Hahn

Futurists can practice their profession in teams or go virtually solo; trend forecaster Haysun Hahn does both. Employing only two assistants in her studio, Hahn is a globetrotter, consulting for more than twenty-five diverse companies worldwide. Her first fashion client was Federated Department Stores in 1990; her list now includes the Gap, Felissimo, Escada, Adidas, Samsung, L'Oreal, and Philips. Hahn was born in Korea, raised in East Africa, and spent her teens in the United States. She capitalizes on her international background and the fact that she is not bound by a native culture, saying that she does not see the world in "segmented orders."

Hahn also runs Futuremode, a creative think tank, and a trend service division, Bureau de Style, that employs about twenty and serves about five hundred clients. The two companies are run from offices in New York City. Hahn has built a significant reputation advising major manufacturers on everything from new sneaker shapes to emerging synthetic textures. "We come up with the main railroad track that everyone will run on," she explains. Hahn's Futuremode clients receive a tailor-made presentation that involves a marketing and cultural analysis; her Bureau de Style clients receive a seasonal color card, newsletter, and group presentation. She repudiates the idea of a crystal ball, relying instead on copious field research into popular culture. For example, she has noticed that, in a time-pressured, travel-based culture, all-in-one products and kits are popular. Such analyses underlie her practical advice on marketing. Hahn can predict how tastes will shift as much as five years in advance. She believes that many in the design industry sense these modulations; however, they may not be as adept at conceptualizing them: "I don't think I'm alone; I just think I'm probably a better communicator—and my antennae may be a bit higher."

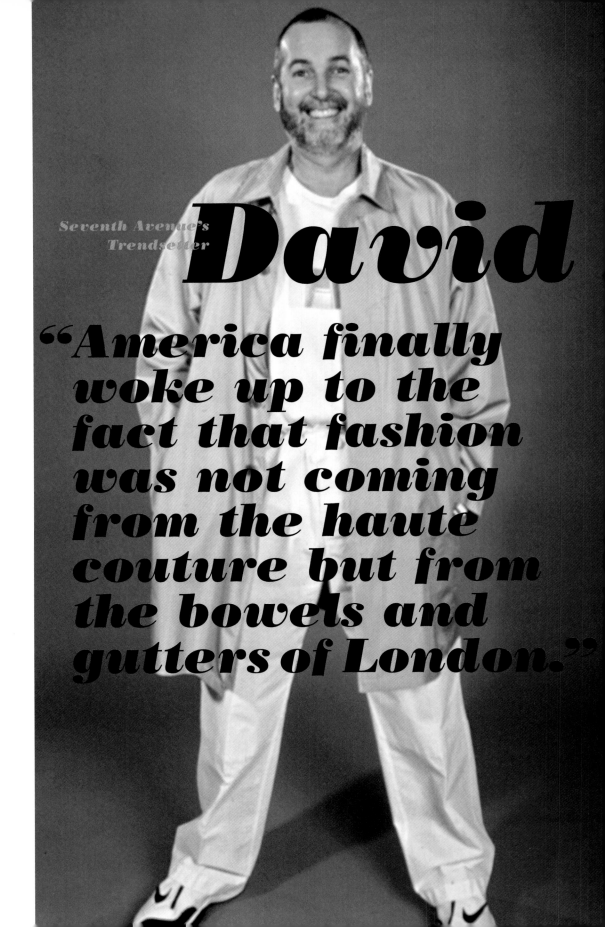

Seventh Avenue's
Trendsetter

David

"America finally woke up to the fact that fashion was not coming from the haute couture but from the bowels and gutters of London."

While most eyes are focused on the next season, David Wolfe is staring down the year 3000. As the head of D3, the trend-forecasting division of the Doneger Group—a venerable Seventh Avenue consulting firm— Wolfe advises mainstream labels such as Ellen Tracy and Estee Lauder, as well as fashion directors like Joan Kaner of Neiman Marcus, about future fashion trends. Prominent among D3's approximately 1,500 fashion clients are names ranging from Nordstrom to Wal-Mart, stores with huge private-label manufacturing arms. Leading Seventh Avenue designers would never admit to buying information from D3, since they employ their own creative staffs to spot trends and forecast. But buy they do, because D3 offers an outsider's objectivity. Wolfe has predicted such major trends as the lingerie look and the Wonderbra, the platform shoe and the rumpled denim revival, and he heralded the ascendance of marketing over design.

Wolfe grew up in Ohio and moved to London in 1968, when he was twenty-seven. The late 1960s was a momentous time for fashion in London, and Wolfe was caught up in the swinging frenzy of Carnaby Street. "Suddenly everyone who knew that Mary Quant's boutique was hot was desperate to find out what would happen next," he recalls. Wolfe's reportage consisted of fashion illustrations for *Women's Wear Daily* and the London *Times*. He was one of the first to spotlight work from Karl Lagerfeld, Jean-Paul Gaultier, and Claude Montana.

Within two years, Wolfe was exporting his fashion savvy. He founded the first trend service to stores in the United States—IM International— with clients Giorgio Armani and Gianni Versace. "America finally woke up to the fact that fashion was not coming from the haute couture but from the bowels and gutters of London," he remembers.

Teenage cool-hunters may recognize fashion when they see it, says Wolfe, but his lectures in Dallas, Los Angeles, New York, and other major fashion capitals initiate fashion trends through his slide shows and pinpoint reporting. Wolfe also waxes poetic about a favorite subject— the experimental clothing laboratory at the Massachusetts Institute of Technology. Based on research from the lab, he predicts a future amalgamation of apparel and technology. "Tattooing and body piercing are the first steps in this transformation," he maintains. In less than a century, Wolfe predicts, fashion will be driven more by innovation provided by technology—heat-sensitive fabrics, holographic prints, computer-generated designs—than by traditional artistry. There will no longer be designers per se—only "technicians," he prognosticates. The very term "designer" will seem archaic.

Sebastien de Diesbach

The reluctant designer turned bureaucrat at the helm of France's industrial trend-forecasting service, Promostyl, is Sebastien de Diesbach. In 1967 his former wife, Danielle, founded the company, and Sebastien helped expand it to London, Tokyo, New York, Sydney, and Helsinki. A former philosophy scholar, de Diesbach is credited with the company's successful transformation from fashion-trend service to industrial product design company. Up to three times a year, teams of product-development executives and creative directors from companies such as Sony, Ray Ban, and Waterman and stores such as Neiman Marcus and Macy's descend on Promostyl's headquarters in the funky eleventh arrondissement of Paris to meet with de Diesbach and his staff of forty trend finders.

Subscribers to Promostyl's fifteen different seasonal publications—notably the "color book" and the "influence book"—number over three thousand.

De Diesbach explains Promostyl's role in the context of a fashion client such as Esprit: "They don't need us to design a specific garment so much as they might need ideas about new markets." From this information, the company might create new directions for materials and silhouettes.

Style-consciousness is an important marketing element for all businesses, and more than half of Promostyl's clients come from outside the fashion industry. The service has long since abandoned its original market niche—the contract textile industry— and now customizes its trend information for a more global clientele, including consumer-goods companies such as electronic-appliance and automobile manufacturers like Casio, Subaru, and Toyota.

Lifestyle-based marketing companies such as computer and appliance manufacturers test new campaigns and shift into new areas by examining what works in the fashion world; clothing is the laboratory for their designs. "Garments will always be in the avant-garde of the trends because they are easier to make," says de Diesbach. The rage for transparency is a perfect example of the way fashion forges the way for other consumer products. Promostyl predicted that translucent, veiled looks would be a big success in ready to wear—as the iMac shows it is equally popular for computers.

"Garments will always be in the avant-garde of the trends because they are easier to make."

tang & tang

little Tang

"MADE IN CHINA"

The Trend Spotters: Scouting the Trends

Once a concept is firmly in mind, a designer draws a croquis (the standard elongated fashion figure) and then cuts out, like so many paper dolls, the multiple sketches needed for the storyboard—a poster-sized assemblage of swatches, magazine pages, yarn tufts, photos of vintage looks. Much of this is now done on computer. At this point the idea must be made real by selecting a season's color palette, choice of fabrics, and detailing.

The decision as to how best to fabricate a designer's sketches is crucial, since the designer must keep abreast of new fabrics in many trade forums around the world. Milan-based Angelo Uslenghi visits New York several times a year to lead fabric shows highlighting the latest trends from Italy's premiere textile mills. At Material World in Miami Beach, Kevin Knaus determines the season's key textures. Instinctive style-finders like Anna Corrina Sellinger dust off vintage items from flea markets around the globe; these elements will inspire new looks for preeminent designers. Lisa Herbert, under the aegis of her company Pantone, the world's leading color consultant, bombards designers with color prognostications, directions about nuance and shade, and even colors coded to coordinate with designers' fabric and notions suppliers, right down to numbered magic markers. The difference between one shade and the next can have a surprising impact on sales.

"Color inspires us and makes us feel, and makes us buy!" *Lisa*

Engineer of Global Color System

Herbert

No businesspeople understand the power of color more than the family dynasty that runs Pantone. Everywhere in the international world of fashion, the universal Pantone color-numbering system enables everyone to speak the same language: no more Tower of Babel in the world of color. "We have 1,757 colors that we deliver to 250,000 major retailers, design labels, and mills," states Lisa Herbert. She has led Pantone into the fashion world, following in the footsteps of her father, Larry Herbert Sr., who in the 1950s used his chemistry background to single-handedly systematize color selection—he was determined to number every hue and tone. In the 1960s, color confusion was rampant in the fashion world: a designer in England would call a textile mill in India asking for a specific color— the red of Diana Vreeland's living room walls, perhaps. But the translation was impossible, so pants did not match jackets and zippers were often just a shade off from the rest of the garment's color.

The Pantone Matching System created order from this chaos in the form of a single color language. Today, designers rely on Pantone color samples to order buttons from the Far East, fabric from France, leather from Italy, and zippers from the United States or Japan. The color-by-number system cuts across all vendor and product lines. Herbert *fille* has taken her father's creation further. In 1983 she and her brother Richard created the Pantone Textile System. Buoyed by her success in the fabric world, Herbert then masterminded the marketing of Pantone as a brand, as a color authority. She founded the Pantone Color Institute and the Pantone Color Awards and then took a plunge into sponsoring the New York City fashion shows. The company even sells agendas in their numbered colors. Of her recent launch of Pantone's forecast office in Milan, she notes, "We work a year to eighteen months in advance to project color trends. Color inspires us and makes us feel, and makes us buy!"

PETERSOM

FALL 2001

For Fall 2001 the color message from designers is clear – the classic and the unexpected make a beautiful pair. This season, designers have combined colors of simple sophistication with hints of bold brashness to create collections that evoke moods of quiet solitude and surprising energy. Rich, chocolatey browns, simple grays, earthy greens, deep blues and warm, creamy neutrals set off shades of striking fuchsia, deep violet and radiant red. With the modern woman as a constant inspiration, designers unapologetically get back to basics to highlight their vision of color in today's world.

Whether inspired by eras past or society today, the Fall 2001 collections are a veritable landscape of color and color combinations. Imagine the soft brown of a vast desert interrupted by the shocking rose of a morning sunrise or the earthy green of the forest floor running into a lake of the deepest indigo. The Fall 2001 vision is one in which colors work together in sophisticated harmony – they sing, they don't shout.

A combination of classic chic and carefree whimsy, the look for Fall 2001 is a powerful statement of uninhibited elegance and femininity. Gone are the days of combining colors unabashedly – this season, a diverse palette of subdued colors with the occasional bright accent rules the runways where sophisticated dressing is the name of the game.

As the official color authority for Fashion Week, Pantone surveys all participating designers to find the most directional colors of the season. The consensus for Fall 2001 is:

Wood Violet	PANTONE	19-3325 TC
Mosstone	PANTONE	17-0525 TC
Fuchsia Rose	PANTONE	17-2031 TC
Hot Chocolate	PANTONE	19-1325 TC
Doe	PANTONE	16-1333 TC
Cardinal	PANTONE	18-1643 TC
Dark Denim	PANTONE	19-4118 TC
Neutral Gray	PANTONE	17-4402 TC

For more information on Fall 2001 color, noted color psychologist Leatrice Eiseman and trend expert Lisa Herbert will both be on hand during Fashion Week for interviews and to provide in-depth color analysis.

PETERSOM

colors: elegant neutrals – gray flannel, multiple shades of brown (chocolate, nutria, mahogany and java), tonic and oyster tan; eclectic "off" colors in avocado green, plum purple, orchid pink, celery; black and white
inspiration: my college years in Connecticut – a mix of Greenwich carpool moms via the nonchalant chic of Marisa Berenson
signature color: chocolate with warm red undertones
color philosophy: menswear classics tossed together with uncontrived feminine flourishes

PANTONE 17-2031 TC **Fuchsia Rose**	PANTONE 19-1325 TC **Hot Chocolate**	PANTONE 16-1333 TC **Doe**

■ **CALVIN**KLEIN

■ **RALPH**LAUREN

CALVINKLEIN

colors: a signature palette of graphic contrast that complements. A range of deep blues – gray-blues, blue-blacks, red-blues

PANTONE 17-0525 TC Mosstone	
PANTONE 19-1325 TC Hot Chocolate	**PANTONE 19-4118 TC** Dark Denim
PANTONE 19-3325 TC Wood Violet	**PANTONE 17-4402 TC** Neutral Gray

Angelo

"The weavers are so advanced that they give ideas to the designers."

Uslenghi

*Italy's Fabric
Forecaster*

Former fabric technician and current spokesperson for the Italian Trade Commission, Angelo Uslenghi is the veritable front line of textile trends. He does not work with finished products but with the threads, yarns, and fibers that make up the textiles. For more than a decade, the Italian Trade Commission has employed Uslenghi to invent new methods of weaving and patterning fabrics and to travel around the world—to Brazil, Singapore, and the United States—to extol the wonders of luxurious and highly manipulated Italian fabrics.

"Because of the success of the Italian style in the 1970s, designers often knew Italian fashion but not the fabrics," recalls Uslenghi, explaining the need for an ambassador of Italian fabrics and yarns. During the late 1970s, he became a messiah, briefing the mills on trends and helping textile designers bridge important gaps so that a consistent message was communicated. For instance, if a designer asked for shine, Uslenghi would instruct the mills to weave the shiny thread Lurex into some of their materials.

Early in his career, the Milan-based Uslenghi linked Dupont—pioneer of man-made fabrics such as nylon— with designers including Valentino in Rome, Emilio Pucci in Florence, and Krizia in Milan. He also taught textile mills such as Ratti, Loro Piano, and Dondi how to brand themselves. Designers and manufacturers now pay a premium for fabrics produced by certain brand-name mills; they have cachet that translates into cash. And some mills now play an important role in trendsetting. According to Uslenghi, "The mills have surpassed the designers. The weavers are so advanced that they give ideas to the designers. The pupils have become more astute than their teachers."

Kevin

In 2000 Material World made its debut in Miami, and all eyes were trained on Kevin Knaus, its creative director. Urban Exhibitions and Fairchild—the fashion media group acquired by Condé Nast in 1999—created this behemoth textile and trim show, which intends to compete stitch for stitch with the well-established European textile shows. American manufacturers have long yearned for a U.S.-based show, and clothing makers eagerly embraced the idea of keeping their design teams on American soil. The organizers tapped Knaus to roam the globe for shocking and innovative ways to display and organize fabric trends that would be on a par with the European shows, since it is as much for trends as for fabrics that designers visit Europe. Now, however, Material World has become an equally important stop on designers' routes around the world.

Material World is not a conventional trade show. It is an experience, an event. At the epicenter of the vast space is Knaus's so-called trend cen-

Knaus

Audiovisual presentations explain the exhibit so that designers can "experience the fabric."

ter, a futurist zone with trends and trimmings arranged by color. Audiovisual presentations explain the exhibit so that designers can, in Knaus's words, "experience the fabric." Around the perimeter of the convention center, fabric vendors are organized by category and color.

Knaus earned his organizational stripes as the former creative director for the Bobbin Show, America's leading sewing- and cutting-machine show, held annually in Atlanta. There he launched the first national student fashion show to give budding designers an industry-wide audience for their work. Simultaneously, he inaugurated the first web site for fashion students, well before the Internet became widely used. On the site, Knaus provides show schedules, backstage information, and networking and job-search leads. Thus the aficionado who tried to match students to dream jobs actually attracted the attention of the leading fashion media company, which pressed him into service.

Anna

Corrina Sellinger

From flea market to high fashion—that is the trend that Anna Corrina Sellinger has observed firsthand and, to some extent, helped author. She has manned a booth at the world-famous Twenty-sixth Street flea market in New York and at the annual Manhattan Antique Textiles Fair—a favorite of designers—since the mid-1990s. When she is not behind the table, Sellinger goes on expeditions with fashion stylists from the top magazines: "We go out and find lost pieces of treasure."

Such treasures include dusty purses, like the handbag that a corporate scout found to inspire Fendi's much-touted "baguette" bag; the bag launched Fendi's revival and ultimate sale for $200 million. Designers and stylists are smitten with Sellinger's discoveries, and she constantly sees elements from her foraging expeditions in designers' collections. Sellinger prefers to keep her designer clientele anonymous, but she notes, "Fendi's secret style-spy has shopped me for years. I also do a lot with Donna Karan—clothes and accessories. She even puts vintage pieces into her Madison Avenue store, so I sell vintage to them as well as inspirational pieces."

Her work as the dig-master for other designers has led her to create her own line of accessories made with antique fabrics. Her gift for fashion archaeology turns past successes—and misses—into today's hits. Sellinger promotes the values of quality craftsmanship and intricate artisanship, as she did while sparking a furor for oversize framed and needlepoint bags. "I see a need for people to express themselves in an increasingly unique way," she says. "With all the technology there is a tendency for sameness. People are in a revolution against the mainstream."

> "I see a need for people to express themselves in an increasingly unique way."

The Visual Messengers: Shaping the Trends

Tantalizing the public with a new fashion message requires the visual talents of art directors, illustrators, and creative directors. The visual stimuli provided by this diverse group of fashion professionals do not serve only to convey a designer's message; a cross-pollination is at work in this area of design. Ruben Toledo's whimsical watercolors and evocative mannequins for Pucci, Harold Koda's groundbreaking museum shows, Bridget de Socio's award-winning layouts, and Anneliese Estrada's creative direction for charity fashion shows: all of this visual information conjures fashion's ever-changing mood.

It is difficult to believe that fashion's most intellectual graphic designer went to school for animal husbandry and started her career in the fashion industry by creating an American flag out of caviar for a *Town & Country* spread. With her avant-garde taste, Bridget de Socio is today best known for art-directing and designing the covers of *Paper* magazine. Many of her provocative covers stand out: Naomi Campbell as Pocahontas in a beaded bikini for a swimsuit issue, a close-to-naked Sandra Bernhard in a Statue of Liberty stance with a raised menorah. "My approach is to do scantily clad content with style," she comments.

De Socio is a fan of the computer graphics that have changed art direction. An early tech enthusiast, she is dismissive of old guard designers who avoid the digital world: "They shouldn't complain about it conceptually if they don't know how to use it. If you've ever played an instrument, it sounds awful before it sounds good. That's what a computer is like." However, de Socio doesn't come to the game armed only with a techno-arsenal. She was legendary for her design expertise in the days of manual page layout. "In the early days, I was known for my surgical hand. I would do all this lettering in perspective and strip it in by hand. It was so precise that the printers couldn't find the seams," she says.

De Socio's Times Square design studio, Socio X, works for many other clients, including Vera Wang. For a recent catalog de Socio used technology to create the same effect as her early handwork. She translated the signature sheer fabric that Wang calls "illusion" into its see-through paper equivalent—vellum. She printed the front of the gown on vellum; the back of the gown, printed on the following page, was visible so that the customer could see both sides. She wanted the catalog viewer to perceive the clothing as she does, in layers. It was technically adroit and visually ethereal—very much like de Socio herself.

Bridget de

"My approach is to clad content with

**Avant-Garde
Graphic Designer**

TETRIS

TETRIS
TOP BY
THIERRY
MUGLER

cyber

Cyber
catsuit by
Jean-Paul
Gaultier

Socio

*do scantily
style."*

CHECKERBOARD

Dress by Versus by Gianni Versace

NAME
THAT
GAME

Photographed by Judson Baker for Jordan Reps

Concept and styling by Stefan Campbell for Marek, NYC

GO RICKI!

PAPER

PAPER

E FASH

our
sizzling
SWIMSUIT
ISSUE
WILL
make
YOU
WET

N BAILEY

HY, TRENDY & CLASSIC THINGS TO DO IN N.Y.C.

LE?

*The Fashion World's
Favorite Illustrator*

Ruben

Fine artist, sculptor, illustrator, and jack of all fashionable trades, Ruben Toledo looms large in what is understood as modern style. He works tirelessly at his passion, creating provocative fashion statements in the most diverse media. His wife—and muse—Isabel Toledo works alongside Ruben. She is a designer's designer who possesses a remarkable facility for traditional dressmaking skills.

Ruben Toledo notes that his career has been largely unplanned. "Isabel and I never thought about a career. We just followed our noses and did what we loved," he says. Isabel worked on textile restoration as an intern at the Costume Institute under Diana Vreeland; Ruben joined Simon Doonan and Katell le Bourhis in the legendary designer and curator's corps of youthful admirers. "She

"The thinking that fashion must change every six months is itself so old-fashioned."

Toledo

enjoyed and cultivated us," he recalls fondly. Vreeland's recruits would go on to preeminent positions in the fashion world.

The Toledos drew guests as diverse as Andy Warhol, the formidable Fendi sisters, and Barneys executives to their shared studio in the epicenter of presanitized Times Square. Ruben Toledo then created for Barneys—and

his old friend Simon Doonan—a series of infamous, satirical zodiac windows. After that display, Annie Flanders at *Details* magazine gave Toledo the back page every month from 1985 to 1990. His ironic cartoons on political and social issues became the Daumiers of the fashion world, wry, funny, and insightful. His signature illustrations for the fashion-oriented Daily Candy web site continue in the same vein.

Toledo is most known for the mannequins he created for the Pucci Company. "In 1985 the style was big-shouldered, mannish, and Isabel made soft, feminine clothing. When

the supermodels came, the clothes weren't displayed on the right body type," he recalls. "I created these feminine forms for her clothes. Now we have a size-sixteen mannequin— and she's a beauty. She's got a real woman's shape, and everyone falls in love with her. The beauty of life is the variety of women." He is sincere in his love of the female form, yet the Toledo style, described as surreal, iconoclastic, and sexy, is indefinable. "We think we're being minimal and clear and plain, but because it is baroque and has so many layers it endures, and that gives us a certain confidence that we didn't have. What we did years ago is still very alive. The thinking that fashion must change every six months is itself so old-fashioned. We are into forever-ness thinking," says Toledo. That type of thinking was on display in the major retrospective of the Toledos' work at the Fashion Institute of Technology in 2000.

Anneliese

Anneliese Estrada has enjoyed a remarkably varied career in the design world. In the early 1980s, she met renowned designer Angel Estrada through his sister, Anneliese's lover at the time. Angel and Anneliese soon married—she wanted to become a United States citizen—and then she took on the merchandising and promotion of his fledgling Estrada label. Soon Angel was fashion's newest darling. Tragically, he was also one of the industry's earliest AIDS casualties.

Anneliese's creative energies did not wane after Angel's death. She began working for *Out* magazine. Her all-lesbian fashion editorial for the gay-oriented *Out* was known for provocative visuals and controversial content. "It was the first time you could actually see real people in layouts, reflecting the culture and who we were. It was a moment in fashion," she recalls. Estrada is credited for single-handedly inventing lesbian chic. "I wanted to create a beautiful world for the often disenfranchised," she

and Blue" compact disk—the first CD to benefit AIDS, with artists such as Annie Lennox and Bono covering Cole Porter classics. The disk was a huge success, giving hope to an industry scarred by the disease.

DIFFA is now Estrada's permanent home. As its creative director, she is both innovator and oracle. Dining by Design, an ongoing show that travels nationally, presents lavishly decorated tables by designers such as Calvin Klein and Tom Ford. With Collection

Estrada

"I wanted to create a beautiful world for the often disenfranchised."

explains. It was not fashion extremism for shock effect but rather evangelism for the marginalized.

Estrada also devoted her formidable energy to DIFFA, the Design Industries Foundation Fighting AIDS. She enlisted friends such as Jean-Paul Gaultier and Rifat Ozbeck to design a trendy collection to accompany the landmark "Red, Hot,

Rouge she inspires designers to push the fashion envelope. For instance, she sent several top designers an ice bucket and challenged them to personalize the contents. Her Canine Couture show presents doggie outfits from Donna Karan and other Seventh Avenue stars. So far, Estrada and DIFFA have raised over $10 million from the fashion industry, and they're still counting.

Fashion connoisseur Harold Koda is the Metropolitan Museum of Art's prodigal son. His first stint there was in the 1970s, when he interned for famed former *Vogue* editor and early Costume Institute director Diana Vreeland. She taught Koda how to make shows that would be "expressive and compelling to the public" in an arena thought to be tired and fusty. Vreeland made theater: as Koda recalls, "The curators would be directing the dressers, and Mrs. V would rescind an order. 'Higher, higher, higher,'" she would say with no concern about making adjustments for the contemporary eye.

Koda took over the helm of the Costume Institute along with his legendary cocurator Richard Martin in 1993. The two met in graduate school at New York University's Institute of Fine Arts and started to work as a curatorial team in the mid-1980s at the Fashion Institute of Technology. Many in the fashion world wondered whether Martin and Koda could fill Vreeland's polished pumps; she was more impresario than academic. However, the curatorial duo had the intellectual authority to elevate fashion to the status of art. "Richard was so engaged in contemporary culture," recalls Koda. "He understood the meaning of what was happening this instant and could show its connection to the past. He would see in Madonna's corset the history of the undergarment back to Marie Antoinette. Richard understood that when contemporary culture becomes enriched by the past, the past becomes less dusty."

Martin and Koda pioneered the role of fashion as social commentary and political expression. At the Met they tapped the pulse of the fashion community, examining its fetishes in shows both controversial and popular: "Fashion and Surrealism," "Splash," "Jocks and Nerds." Martin published over one hundred scholarly papers and several books; he died of cancer at fifty-two. Shortly before Martin's death, Koda went to the Harvard University Graduate School of Design to study landscape architecture; he also cocurated the Guggenheim Museum's blockbuster Armani retrospective. Now he has once again returned to the Costume Institute, where he strives to make what could be a dry academic experience into Broadway spectacle. An upcoming exhibition like "Xtreme Beauty," featuring foot-binding, Burmese neck rings, and eighteenth-century panniers, shows "how the past resonates in our lives." The elements "deform and reform" the body's inherent contours.

The mirror that Koda trains on the fashion world also reflects back. While the public gazes at vitrines in the exhibitions, designers from around the world visit the Costume Institute's exceptional archive; elements from a vintage Paco Rabanne or Balenciaga garment might inform a contemporary collection. The Costume Institute started in 1937 with two thousand pieces and now includes eighty thousand items; the annual benefit gala hosted by Koda fuses the demimonde of the fashion world with the New York social scene.

Harold Koda

*Curator Combining
Fashion and Scholarship*

"When contemporary culture becomes enriched by the past, the past becomes less dusty."

The Muses: Inspiring the Design

A muse is the mirror that reflects a designer's idealized vision. Audrey Hepburn, in her half-century relationship with couturier Hubert de Givenchy, was the first recognized muse. Today's muse has an especially dynamic role. No longer a celebrity mannequin, the contemporary muse may be lured into the corporate fold as a working member of the design team, like Victoire de Castellane. Some designers make their muse a part of their inner circle; Amanda Harlech and Karl Lagerfeld maintain a nonstop dialogue. And sometimes the muse is an advocate catapulting a designer into business, as Isabella Blow has done for many young, avant-garde talents.

Isabella
Blow

Nurturer of
Young Designers

David La Chapelle

The style maven Isabella Blow sets off a whirlwind of flashbulbs every time she steps into a fashion crowd. She is unashamed of her outrageous fashion personality. It is one of the reasons she continually sniffs out new talent like Givenchy's head designer, the iconoclast Alexander McQueen. "A muse has many different functions," Blow says. For McQueen, she bought his entire first clothing collection and then invited him to move into her Belgravia home.

"She championed Alexander," says her husband, Detmar Blow, an art and fashion dealer. "She wore his clothes throughout the time she was working at British *Vogue*." During McQueen's stay with Blow and her husband, he became interested in Blow's long-standing passion for things both medieval and Scottish; in fact, he made tartan his signature look. In October 1996, the tremendous press attention McQueen garnered led Bernard Arnault of LVMH Moët Hennessy Louis Vuitton to appoint him to reinvigorate Givenchy.

Today, Isabella Blow, once regarded as an eccentric figure heralding minor, unwearable designers like Philip Treacy, is very much in the mainstream, with other nascent design talents under her wing. She single-handedly persuaded the owner of Brown's (the Barneys of Great Britain) to show Hussein Chalayan's work in the store window. She also persuaded her husband to represent designer Jeremy Scott in France.

Blow herself was discovered in the mid-1980s by the then editor of British *Vogue*, Anna Wintour. "She saw something in me, and I saw something in her," Blow comments. She worked with Wintour to remake the feel of the magazine—showcasing extravagant designers, shooting outdoors in unusual locations, and using outré props. Now it is Blow who is the subject of the camera's lens.

Isabella Blow, once regarded as an eccentric figure, is very much in the mainstream.

Victoire

"Fashion was my milieu."

The famous French fashion muse Victoire de Castellane is known for the spell she casts. She is a veteran of the French fashion scene, providing inspiration to many designers. In addition, she has recently assumed the role of designing the precious jewelry collection for Dior. "I've been in love with jewelry since I was four," she says.

De Castellane has a noteworthy family heritage with deep roots in fashion. Her maternal uncle, Giles de Four, longtime head of Chanel and currently running Balmain, introduced the young de Castellane to fashion, taking her to fittings and shows at Chanel. Her father's godmother was Barbara Hutton, also an early influence. "Fashion was my milieu. Barbara was my grandmother's best friend, and she wore big, beautiful jewelry. She was my muse and the reason that I love fun fashion."

Although de Castellane started her career working at Chanel at the age of twenty, her current inspiration is the house of Dior, with its emblematic flower and enigmatic star designer, John Galliano. Many in the industry claim Galliano poached de Castellane; she is more likely to say she is following her own muse.

de Castellane

Perhaps there is no designer more associated with his muse than Karl Lagerfeld, the uber-designer for Chanel, with the British beauty Amanda Harlech. As Lagerfeld and other couture designers became increasingly aware of Great Britain's new fashion leadership, the muses were not forgotten. Harlech describes her job with Lagerfeld as being his "outside pair of eyes."

But in reality she is much more involved. Harlech travels constantly with Lagerfeld, providing inspiration through her visceral reactions to all that she sees. She is Lagerfeld's visual sounding board for the biannual runway collections he designs for Chanel couture, ready-to-wear, and accessories. She also provides overall direction to licensees and assists Lagerfeld in creating collections for Fendi Furs, as well as his own eponymous line of clothing.

Harlech seems mesmerized by Lagerfeld's working method, expressing amazement at his surfeit of talent. She recalls an advertising shoot in Biarritz, where he not only created the clothes and art-directed the photos but also took the shots: "I watched his fascination with the play of volumes—the petal of a skirt, the sail of a shirt." Harlech helped Lagerfeld translate this idea into a series of drawings. The next season, runways featured models accessorized to represent flowers.

"They had stemlike torsos caught by a wafer-thin band of real gold at the waist," Harlech describes. A month later, designers such as Donna Karan and Calvin Klein had transformed this gold band into a more commercial leather strap—the belted look of the New York shows.

It was not easy for Lagerfeld to pluck Harlech away from the British designer John Galliano, with whom she had worked for twelve years beginning during her days as a fashion editor for *Harper's & Queen* and *Vogue*. But he was determined, and his enthusiasm and persistence have paid off in collections that are consistently acclaimed.

Amanda
Harlech travels constantly with Lagerfeld, providing inspiration through her visceral reactions to all she sees.

Harlech

The Extremists: Striking a Pose

Extremists are like muses, but they are not tethered to a single designer; they attract the attention of the entire fashion industry with outrageous attire, makeup, and antics. At every fashion soiree, the extremists are photographed by the paparazzi for their theatrics as much as for their embodiment of the season's looks. Fashion's risk-takers include Lauren Ezersky: one of her on-air escapades was a romp around Bergdorf with John Galliano. Patrick McDonald attracts open-mouthed stares with, for instance, his Oswald Botang redingote. The runway is often accused of being an idealized environment of transparent tops and hobbling skirts, and the party arena is one step further away from fashion reality. *Visionaire* goes yet another step, publishing the most esoteric distillations of fashion photography. Designers take notes from these playbooks—and from the postures of the partygoers at each issue launch. They are the living caricatures of the fashion world.

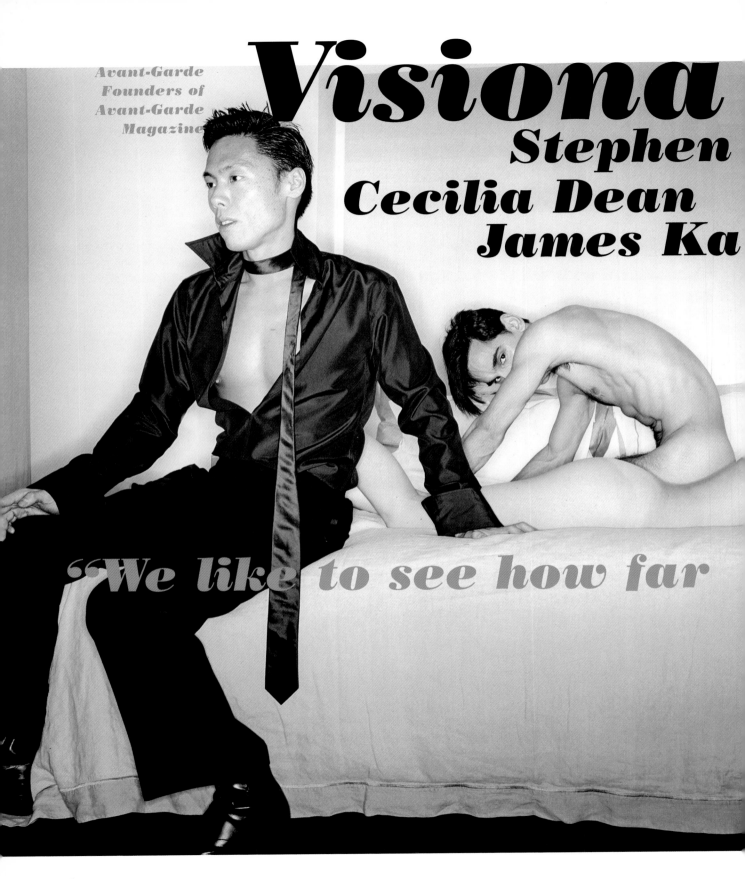

Visiona
Stephen
Cecilia Dean
James Ka

"We like to see how far

ire
Gan
liardos

The austere space in a building south of Houston Street in New York City resembles a gallery, but it is actually the publishing headquarters of *Visionaire*. The offices hum with energy, and in the center of the cool space are three identical desks lined up with Euclidean precision. Here sit the three founders of *Visionaire*, erstwhile high school buddies turned fashion revolutionaries Cecilia Dean, Stephen Gan, and James Kaliardos.

The first issues of the fashion and art magazine mysteriously appeared at newsstands and bookstores in Soho. Now the magazine has over six thousand subscribers, many of whom rank among the industry's elite. *Visionaire* is more fashion happening or object than magazine. One "issue" might include a collection of photos of nude models snapped by Karl Lagerfeld or a light box designed by Tom Ford of Gucci

Visionaire fills a gaping void in the fashion industry: it provides an excitement and a fresh aesthetic reminiscent of Richard Avedon's work at *Vogue* in the 1960s. "It's a gallery in print," proclaims the magazine's lanky cofounder Stephen Gan. He and his partners, who started *Visionaire* in 1991, comment, "We like to see how far we can go with an idea." The young trio responded to the fashion scene with a new type of media; unique in the magazine industry is the irregular publishing schedule. "We experimented with the light box issue for nine months," says makeup artist and stylist James Kaliardos. To meet the demands of their expanding subscriber base they created the slick *V*, edited by Alix Brown.

Cecilia Dean, the muse of *Visionaire*, attends fashion shows wearing garments that represent the fashion of

we can go with an idea."

that provides a viewing station for accompanying homoerotic transparencies (including an infamous anatomical close-up of Alexander McQueen). In August 1996, *Visionaire* 18 attracted the immediate attention of Seventh Avenue. A monogrammed Louis Vuitton envelope contained provocative fashion and photography—the two engines of *Visionaire*'s turbo thrust.

the moment, or the soon-to-be moment. This former model eschews the status of fashion's "it girl," preferring to concentrate on the photographers she discovers. In fact, *Visionaire* cites as the core of its philosophy the promotion of fashion photography as art; its success in this area has been noticed by the Museum at the Fashion Institute of Technology, which in 2001 mounted a retrospective of *Visionaire*'s art photography and specialty issues.

VISIONAIRE

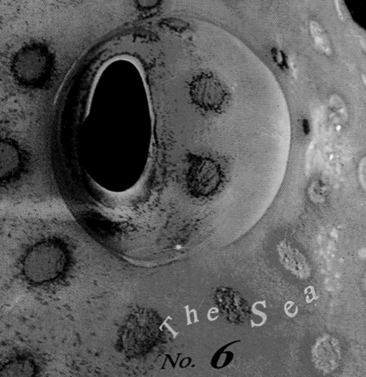

No. *1*

SPRING 1991

VISIONAIRE

SUN BEAMS

VISIONAIRE

The Sea

No. *6*

No. *4*

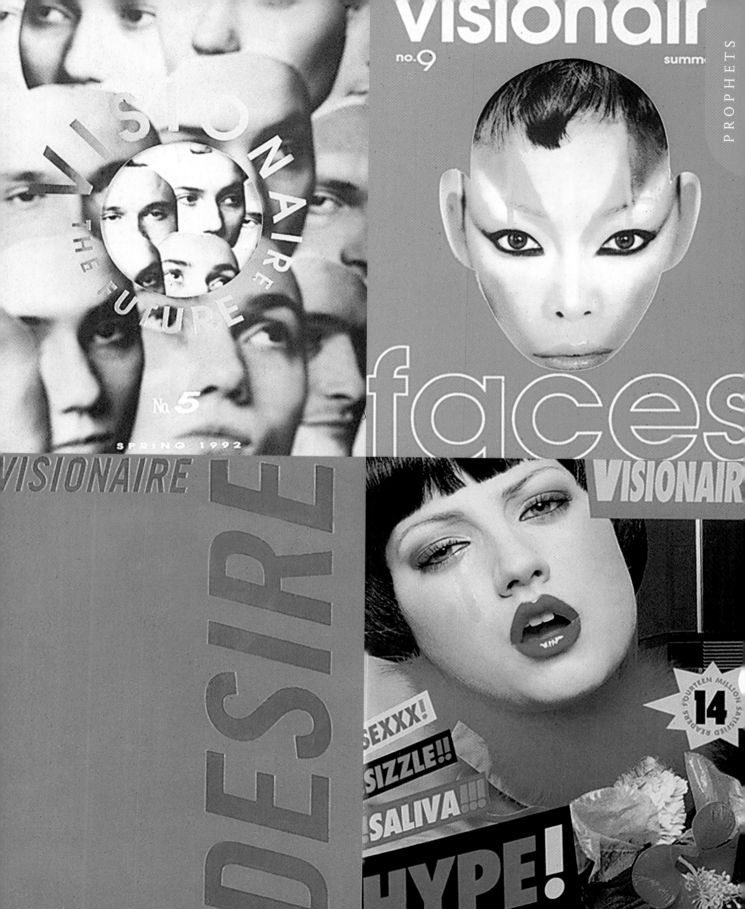

visionair
no.9   summ
PROPHETS

faces

VIS
NAIRE
THE FUTURE
No. 5
SPRING 1992

VISIONAIRE   DESIRE   VISIONAIR

SEXXX!
SIZZLE!!
SALIVA!!!
HYPE!

FOURTEEN MILLION SATISFIED READERS
14

Television's Defiant
Fashion Host

Lauren

Ezersky

The famous television show "Behind the Velvet Ropes" has been on the air since 1984, thanks to the tenacity of its eccentric host, Lauren Ezersky. Launched by onetime *New York* magazine writer Earl Crittenden as a culture, fashion, and entertainment show with in-depth interviews of designers and behind-the-scenes reporting on fashion and trunk shows, "Behind the Velvet Ropes" was a cable success in New York in the 1980s. Ezersky, a guest who soon shared the microphone with Crittenden, took control of the show in the 1990s, adding her own funky couture style to the original New York club-kid emphasis. E! Entertainment Television acquired the show for itself and its offshoot, Style, in 1999, and "Behind the Velvet Ropes" is now broadcast internationally.

Ezersky handles the byzantine tasks of producing, directing, and hosting each show. While the program is popular, she must continually battle the network executives who keep it in narrow distribution. "I was in Palm Beach, and all these matrons came up to me, asking for my autograph. It was amazing that they were fans, but the producers still think I'm too New York," she notes. "I want to take the show more mainstream but not lose my individuality. That's the hardest thing for me to prove to the producers. I want to dress the way I dress, talk the way I talk, be who I am. I can't stand it when everyone is so homogenized."

"I can't stand it when everyone is so homogenized."

film and fashion
with the stars of the silverscreen

The Fashion Group International® invites you to join them for the 16th Annual Night of Stars

...an Oscar-worthy evening honoring those Hollywood stars, designers and makeup artists who made the movies the most important fashion influence of the 20th Century

Honorees

Superstar Award:
Nino Cerruti

Corporate Award:
Hal Rubenstein, for IN STYLE

Edith Head Award:
Ann Roth

Humanitarian Award:
Lord & Taylor

Night of Stars Award:
Badgley Mischka
Angela Bassett
Max Factor
Ali MacGraw
Vera Wang

Tuesday, October 26, 1999
The Rainbow Room
30 Rockefeller Plaza
Black Tie
6:30 p.m. – Cocktails
7:30 p.m. –dinner and awards
ceremony followed by Wrap Party 9:30
champagne, dessert and dancing

Honorary Chair:
Fred Hayman

Creative Committee:
Diane Clehane, Madeline DeVries, Louise Evins, Julie Kagel,
Edie Locke, Richard Lambertson, Lisa Lori, Marylou Luther,
Kate McEnroe, Janet Mick, Bernadine Morris, Amy Rosi

Sponsors:
American Movie Classics
Givaudan-Roure Corporation
Procter & Gamble
Time Inc.
Webcraft Technologies, Inc.

Design and
Illustration by
Ruben Toledo
Graphic Design
by Harry Lee

Divas and dandies must, as a rule, cultivate an exaggerated style—at various events they must be noticed cutting a swath through quotidian trends. Patrick McDonald revels in his dandy status. He dons the latest and most outlandish looks and identifies with other celebrities who appreciate costume. "I'm not into clone dressing—I don't need to fit in," declares McDonald.

McDonald and his identical twin, Michael, have always been obsessed by fashion. When he was a child, McDonald would be outfitted in white eyelet shirts, royal-blue velvet shorts and suspenders, and white cutout sandals—pure Little Lord Fauntleroy. He notes that the look might appeal to him now: "Velvet is very happening." By seventh grade, the twins were dressed in matching teal Nehru jackets, cigarette pants, and silver medallion necklaces.

"Mom loved I. Magnin's and Gump's, and we were basically raised there until she took us to Europe and we went to the Pucci palace in Florence—God knows how many Pucci dresses she had to buy to ensure that we made it into the palace," recalls McDonald.

After a few years modeling and a short stint at the ultra-hip store Fiorucci—"It was like a club during the day"—McDonald worked at Barneys as it reached its fashion zenith with the opening of the women's store in the mid-1980s. McDonald managed the duplex cocktail and couture departments. "I wore evening for day, Gaultier jackets, polka-dot Manolo Blahnik shoes, and makeup—which did get heavier as my hairline receded," he comments.

Fashion in Film Issue

Jil Sander   Russell Simmons   Cindy Sherman   Cary Grant   Viktor & Rolf   Michel Comte
Okwui Enwezor   Fred Astaire   Christian Louboutin   Plum   Hollywood Young Turks

In 1989 he started a job as design assistant and business manager to the designer Fabrice: "We dressed everyone—Whitney Houston, Natalie Cole, the whole 'Unforgettable' tour." Since 1994, McDonald has been jack-of-all-trades at John Anthony, one of only three remaining couturiers active in America. The detailing—delicate silks, flawless embroidery—and elaborate tailoring of the gowns is the hallmark of extravagant fashion.

Fashion's Provocateur # Patrick

"I'm not into clone dressing—I don't need to fit in."

McDonald

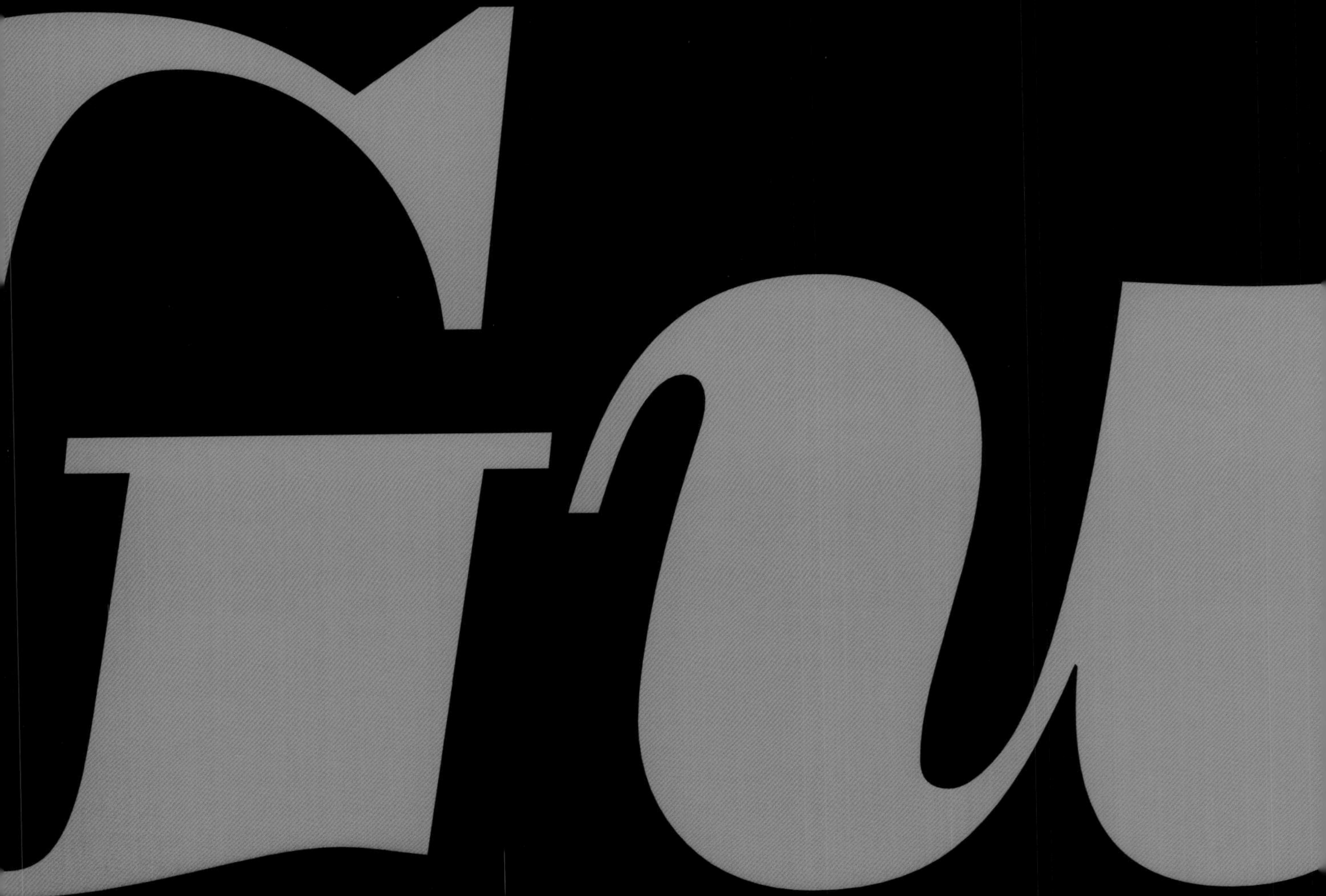

Gurus

The ratio of gurus to prophets is at least three to one. For every fashion soothsayer with a singular message—say, the return to the organic—a slew of savants stands ready to translate its meaning, perhaps in the theater that is a runway presentation or the moody mise-en-scène of fashion photography.

Chief among the gurus are the editors who first hear the message and channel it to the public. These are not wordsmith style editors, jotting with a pencil or tapping on a keyboard. These are editors who scurry from showroom to showroom in the garment center and shop to shop in the city's trendiest neighborhoods. They prowl for the one perfect item to illustrate the newest theme proclaimed by the prophets—a dress with just the right slouch, a jacket with a particular cut. They might even mention to a designer that a certain handbag specially made in pink alligator—instead of the usual printed canvas—would make it into the hands of a celebrity model, onto the pages of the magazine, and into the order books of retail and wholesale customers.

The photographer is equally responsible for formulating the design aesthetic. Whether inventing new sets and poses or selecting a specific look from the most recent collections, the photographers who snap the most intriguing shots hold significant power within the fashion world. The stylist works hand in hand with the photographer to arrange every element of a fashion shoot.

Fashion's sine qua non is the runway show, replete with stick-thin models strutting down paper-lined catwalks. The fashion show has a cast of thousands—producer, make-up artists, prop handlers, and more—and the importance to the brand and the complexity of the presentation belie its brief duration.

Gauging these editorial looks with eagle-eyed canny are the promoters and publicists. These public relations professionals are the enthusiastic marketers who find ways to attract editorial interest in various products. Free exposure in magazines is as valuable as high-priced advertisements, and these promoters ensure that key magazine editors are sitting in the right seats at the runway shows, that black-and-white images are sent instead of color when appropriate, and that various corporate sponsors will help pack a goody bag. In short, they know how to throw a great party without losing sight of their clients.

The retail store remains the focus for both wholesale and retail merchants. From marketing to window display to dressing-room drama, all energies are concentrated on a single result: a customer laden with status shopping bags. This corps of professional hustlers depends on just one transaction: turning design caprice into retail cash.

The Storytellers: Presenting the Trends

The power of the pen in fashion is absolute. Designers are wont to burst into tears at the smallest scowl that crosses the implacable visage of *Vogue*'s Anna Wintour—let alone an unfavorable review. Fashion editors are near-deities to some aspiring designers, worshipped with precious offerings of samples and prototypes. The designer can never be certain of the editor's caprice.

The fashion editor must interpret the fashion story for its target audience: Emil Wilbekin has overseen the cultification of hip-hop star Mary J. Blige into fashion diva at *Vibe,* while Pamela Fiori has rejuvenated the venerable *Town & Country* to appeal to a young affluent crowd. Through their idiosyncratic choices, editors and writers cast their own spell. A William Norwich, for instance, at the *New York Times* serves as fashion's social critic; *InStyle*'s Hal Rubenstein captures the celebrity-cum-fashionista zeitgeist. Wendy Goodman visits designers' homes in a quest for the nexus of creativity, and Bridget Foley and Dennis Freedman oversee a fashion empire at Fairchild/Condé Nast. The ground troops are the market editors, who constantly patrol showrooms and designer workshops.

Mass-Media
Fashion Critic

Hal Ru

Ever since Greta Garbo donned a man's tuxedo in Weimar Germany, fashion has adored celebrities. When star-studded *InStyle* magazine hit the newsstands in the mid-1990s, it shocked the fashion world. Celebrity dress and lifestyle were the core of its content—Cameron Diaz casual, Jennifer Lopez glam, and Courtney Love polished—and millions of readers were drawn in. Issues of *InStyle* have even outsold *Vogue*. The fashion elite has responded: Gwyneth Paltrow and Oprah Winfrey have knocked supermodels off fashion magazine covers.

Fashion features editor Hal Rubenstein explains, "My job is not to make fashion mysterious but rather to show celebrities as approachable—not as perfect people. We do not deify the celebrities. We show how Tom Hanks looks as a dad. It's about daily life and not being embarrassed about mundanity. The stars are wearing what people are really wearing." While he lassos celebrities every month, he also credits the founding editor: "Mary Peacock was the midwife of the magazine."

In cowboy boots and leather jacket, Rubenstein cuts an imposing figure with his easy, relaxed stride. His voice has the timbre of a cowboy and the inflection of a native New Yorker. His early years were marked by a failed screenplay that left him with decade-long writer's block, but by 1995 a chance meeting with Annie Flanders of *Details* led to his own column, "The Edge of Nightlife." In a short time, Rubenstein had freelanced his way through *New York* magazine, the *New York Times,* and the short-lived Forbes publication *Egg* before landing at *InStyle,* where he exercises both his eye for celebrity style and his penchant for covering it.

"My job is not to make fashion mysterious but rather to show celebrities as approachable."

benstein

William Norwich

Before he became the entertaining editor of the *New York Times Magazine,* William Norwich was already famous as one of the fashion world's funniest columnists. The industry could not stop talking about an article that appeared in the fall 1999 *Fashions of the Times.* Entitled "Billy Makes a Dress," the quirky noisseur. During graduate school he was introduced to Eugenia Sheppard, the legendary fashion columnist for the *Herald Tribune;* along with *W's* John Fairchild, she was the first journalist to write about fashion designers as celebrities. Another introduction was to Earl Blackwell, the founder of Celebrity Service. Norwich wit and bonhomie. He became widely known for his weekly "Style Diary," published in the *New York Observer* from 1993 until 2000. One of his most memorable columns came out in a season in which many European designers showed skirts for men. Norwich wore a different skirt each day for a week and wrote

Norwich is equal parts Ezra Pound and Diana Vreeland.

report described his attempt to design and tailor a dress and then try to sell it to a store buyer. Designers everywhere smiled in empathy at Norwich's travails as his painstakingly designed garment was assessed as "having little hanger appeal."

Norwich's cousin Anne R. "Bunny" Goodman, one of the last of *Vogue's* famous illustrators, provided early inspiration to the budding style con-

helped pen Blackwell's fourth edition of *The Celebrity Register,* a compendium of profiles. By the end of the 1980s, Norwich had written a man-about-town column for the *Daily News* and had become a contributor and then editor-at-large at *Vogue.* He also worked at *House & Garden,* but he was inexorably drawn to fashion as social and historical commentary.

Norwich is equal parts Ezra Pound and Diana Vreeland. The hallmark of a Norwich feature or column is investigative irreverence written with

about people's reactions. He describes a dream assignment: a tour of the president's White House closet: "I'd learn more about the man that way than from listening to a speech." By merging his interests in fashion and home, the closet has become to William Norwich what an annual report is to a business writer—a path into the psyche of his subject.

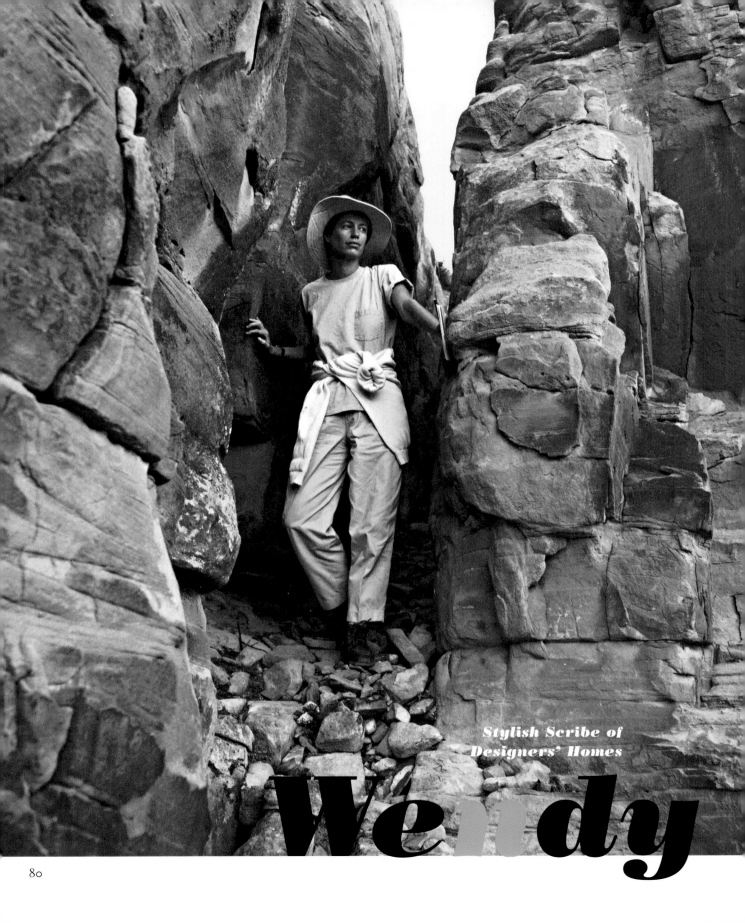

Stylish Scribe of
Designers' Homes

Wendy

Journalist Wendy Goodman has done time at every important fashion and shelter magazine; for several years she has been the home editor of *New York Magazine*. She ferrets out homes with styles that reveal the owners' "interior life." Her groundbreaking coverage for *House & Garden* focused on designers in their environments; Goodman moved beyond the

The perceptive Goodman works mainly through collaboration with her subjects: "I feel genuinely protective. I'm not out to make anyone feel embarrassed." With big-name celebrities, who are often wary of a ruthless press, she attempts a balancing act in what she describes as a "fragile situation with subjects who are intensely private." Goodman

"I look for the soul of the subject."

showroom and right into the bedroom with the personalities she covered. Raiding closets for their real clothes, she was the antithesis of the editors who staged sterile interviews in heavily propped manor houses. Goodman analyzed every detail, like a psychoanalyst of style: "When people see that you're not going to dictate to them and they trust you, then you've got something going."

calms their fears. "I look for the soul of the subject," she says. "Nothing has any meaning unless it is personal. You can decorate a room with all the money in the world, but those environments at the end of the day mean nothing without a point of view." Goodman's unerring focus on her subjects often isolates colors and themes that will appear in future collections. From a Turkish souk aesthetic in a designer's study to a hermetic cell in Barbados, the interior mood shifts onto the storyboard.

Goodman

Vibe, the brainchild of music industry super-producer Quincy Jones and Time Inc.'s Steve Ross, did for the 1990s what *Rolling Stone* did for the 1960s. A monthly glossy started in 1993, *Vibe* holds a mirror to urban culture, politics, music, and fashion—the elements that define an era. Emil Wilbekin, editor-in-chief, was a founding staffer. "Quincy's original idea was that hip-hop was a burgeoning new music form, and all these kids were into it," Wilbekin says. "He just knew it would grow into a culture. Time Inc. believed that, too. Think about what is encompassed by urban music: it's hip-hop, R & B,

dance hall, rap, reggae, and jazz." According to Wilbekin, *Vibe* aspires to "make global and multicultural the fusion of music, politics, fashion, and the arts—everything that is urban."

Wilbekin explains the perception of hip-hop as a movement: "It's growing and creative. It's really changing the face of this country—how we view style and fashion." A former fashion director, he knows the force of the hip-hop influence: "The runways of Europe are all hip-hop and baggy and urban."

Vibe, with a circulation of almost one million, attributes much of its success to being able to parody itself. "We live the culture and we know it changes quickly, so we don't take

ourselves too seriously," confesses Wilbekin. The magazine models itself on the content-driven, celebrity-studded *Vanity Fair* and the erstwhile *Spy;* it also rejects the prevailing view of urban youth as angry and disaffected. Wilbekin keeps current on street looks by dropping in on sporting-goods shops, clubs, and dance hall parties. "The culture is with it," says Wilbekin. "That's why fashion people like *Vibe.*"

Vibe aspires to "make global and multicultural the fusion of music, politics, fashion, and the arts."

Synthesizer of Fashion and Music

Emil

Wilbekin

"The days when you grew into reading **Town & Country** and you had to have the right family and pedigree are gone."

Pamela

The fashion world is sometimes taken aback to discover that the editor-in-chief of *Town & Country*, Pamela Fiori, still pens her own pieces—from a cover feature on Sophia Loren to a travel story on Rajasthan. This incredulity is easy to understand in an industry where stylists pick out tantalizing outfits and *objets* while an entirely different corps of editors is hired for the painstaking task of actually describing them.

When Fiori took the helm of *Town & Country,* the oldest continually published magazine in America, the average age of readers was in the mid-fifties. The whole market of rich older people was almost written off. "When I first became editor, there was an attitude that our readership was irrelevant—that they were dinosaurs and passé," she recalls. But the ascendance of a new moneyed class in the 1990s coupled with a lust for style brought about a shift in the demographics of the typical *Town & Country* reader. Now, the average age of readers is in the mid-forties, and a new ethnic and cultural diversity is visible on every page of the magazine. "There are people from a range of backgrounds who are making a lot of money and living the American dream," Fiori points out. *Town & Country* uses more ethnic models than other glossy magazines, and its society or "parties" page is equally diverse. "The days when you grew into reading *Town & Country* and you had to have the right family and pedigree are gone. Today, the overwhelming majority of the wealth in America is self-made. There is a whole new brand of rich people—from Silicon Valley, Seattle, and other countries," comments Fiori. The magazine speaks for a world—and readership—in transition: "It has changed as dramatically as the web has changed the way we do business."

Fiori waxes enthusiastic about the magazine's success in delivering serious content and style. "It encompasses more than just fashion. It's the art on your walls, it's the books you read, and where you vacation. It's how you live and how you think, and how you dress and what interests you," she explains. When refocusing *Town & Country*, Fiori was determined to isolate what she saw as an emerging new market; instead of plying snobbishness and retreating into an archaic elitism, she reached out. "The fun of editing the magazine is that we don't want to see people with their noses pressed against the glass; we want them to come in," she says. "Buy as much as you want, enjoy as much as you want."

Fiori

**Leading Editor
of Time-Honored
Magazine**

Bridget Foley & Dennis Freedman

Trade Editor
and Creative Director

Moving at a fast clip through the vast warren of open cubicles at Fairchild Publications headquarters in New York, Bridget Foley almost looks like a supermodel herself. She is a real-life symbol of the open and quick-paced trade publication *WWD* (*Women's Wear Daily*) and its upscale sister, the consumer magazine *W*. Foley and creative director Dennis Freedman, under the benign tutelage

lications, including *Footwear News*, *DNR* (*Daily News Record*), and *HFN* (*Home Furnishings News*), Foley notes, "The creative latitude comes straight from the top. One of the things that Patrick McCarthy is remarkable for is that he trusts the writers and editors on the staff. He allows them freedom to experiment, which has led fashion photographers including Mario Testino, Craig McDean, and Juergen

W is a laboratory for the avant-garde, and the team's missionary-like zeal has led to controversial results. In the late 1990s, *W* was pilloried for what appeared to be a promotion of "heroin chic." However, *W* did not intend this depiction of street chic to be cultural commentary or endorsement; it was pure, hard-edged, documentary observation.

"In the grand scheme, fashion provides a way of reading social history."

of Patrick McCarthy (founder John Fairchild's chosen successor), strive for camaraderie with a light-hearted atmosphere that, unlike many in the fashion world, retains devoted employees. Swift, hard-hitting, and indisputably successful (*W*'s ad pages cost more than forty-five thousand dollars), the two publications draw in more than their share of fashion cognoscenti.

Foley and Freedman continually give credit to their team, disclaiming any proprietary responsibility for *W*'s cult status—another unusual trait in an industry long on snobbishness and self-aggrandizement. Of the near-seamless operation of Fairchild and its array of revered fashion trade pub-

Teller to present some of their most personal work. That, in turn, has drawn in photographers from the art world such as Tina Barney and Philip Lorca di Corcia."

The trademarks of both *W* and *WWD* are the well-written essay, coverage of breaking news, and concise reportage; thus the team can afford to be brazen and obsessive in the search for the utmost in scintillating images. Freedman, in his quest for a modern style, is not moved by empty novelty. "One of the most meaningless words to describe fashion photography is 'edgy,'" he says. "'Provocative' isn't new, either. What I look for in photographs is a quality and an honesty, not images that are provocative for the sake of being provocative."

Foley states, "*W*'s editors are passionate about fashion. There are so many levels on which fashion can be enjoyed and deliberated, debated and dissected." In June 2001, the Council of Fashion Designers of America gave Foley its highest honor, the Eugenia Sheppard Award for Fashion Journalism. She reflects, "In the grand scheme, fashion provides a way of reading social history, but in the most basic sense you also have to put on clothes to leave the house. Fashion is the convergence of all kinds of disparate elements—from street culture to rarefied haute couture."

Sasha Charnin Morrison

Rae Ann Scandroli

Ellyn Chestnut

Ashley Kennedy

Robert Beauchamp

Irenka Jakubiak

Mimi Shin

Alice Kim

Heather Bracher Severs

The Pagemakers

Media Talent Scouts

One of the many paradoxes of the fashion industry is that while magazine market editors often travel as a pack each caters to an extremely specific reader demographic and will emerge from a product debut with a different item. From a single fashion presentation, the editors select ensembles or items that have only the label in common. The effect on the visibility of a designer or a look is enormous: when *W* showcases a dropped-waist pant and *Vogue* simultaneously pictures a Daryl K hip-hugger, the waistline of millions of women's trousers drops.

This multiplier effect allows market editors to determine what is hot and what is not. *Elle* magazine's Ellyn Chestnut, for instance, made her mark on fashion by combining elements from a range of categories—hats, bracelets, handbags—to depict a particular look. On a similar high fashion plane are the pages constructed by Mimi Shin of *Harper's Bazaar*. Shin may work the phones for days to find just the right camouflage pieces for a shoot in Manila on military modes. In contrast, a market editor at a younger magazine, such as Ashley Kennedy at *Lucky,* focuses on what retail customers will see in stores that season: the most fashionable bracelets, the most elegant wraps. Meanwhile, Rae Ann Scandroli focuses on *Glamour*'s legendary "Dos and Don'ts."

Heather Bracher Severs of *Town & Country* formulates an iconic look for her accessories pages: to appeal to her upscale market, she will set a single satin clutch on a bed of diamonds. Yet another market editor, *Allure*'s Sasha Charnin Morrison, will draw her readership in with a page on high and low styles featuring a $3900 Hermès Birkin bag alongside a $39 Old Navy look-alike.

Irenka Jakubiak of *Accessories* magazine may act as a senior market editor—prowling the showrooms and runways for every accessory trend from golf socks to Harry Winston parures—but in reality she is the publication's editor-in-chief. *Accessories* is to the trade what *Vogue* is to the public—a monthly bible that covers myriad industries within the fashion marketplace. And Alice Kim at *InStyle* can create a national craze for, say, shoulder-brushing earrings with one cover photo.

Whereas the accessories editors for women's clothing often specialize, men's market editor Robert Beauchamp at *Departures* magazine covers everything from bow ties to bathing trunks. But perhaps times are about to change. By appointing an editor for menswear, the travel-based luxury magazine *American Express* is signaling the growing importance of designer looks for their affluent male readers.

The Stylists: Showcasing the Fashion Story

A stylist is, in many ways, a designer sans label, the unofficial creator of a designer's look on the runway or in the media. The field of styling has only recently come into its own. Stylists are the ultimate multitaskers, juggling four major roles. Master stylists such as Wendy Schecter and L'Wren Scott assist designers in creating complete runway ensembles, down to accessories and other props. Empress of the styling field, Polly Allen Mellen collaborates with editors to produce lush editorial spreads in far-flung locales. Acting as conduit for designers and synthesizing the season's trends for celebrities are Derek Khan and Arianne Phillips. Finally, stylists like Debra McGuire serve as official or unofficial costume designers for looks on screen.

Stylists occupy a unique perch in fashion's pantheon. Designers have not always credited stylists, preferring to appear as if they had not only designed each garment but also coordinated the complete "looks" for the runway shows. Magazines, too, disparaged the stylist: editors laid claim to all the work of a fashion shoot. With the new preeminence of the styling field, these visual editors have come into credits of their own.

Creating a stand-out page in a sea of glamorous magazine spreads takes the trained eye of a seasoned sittings editor. For a photographic shoot, sittings editors—almost as fundamental to a magazine as the editor-in-chief and the creative director—select the model, finalize the clothes, and decide on props, backdrops, and emotional expression.

The images styled by Polly Allen Mellen always make arresting visual statements. She has worked her magic in the industry for over thirty-five years as a star sittings editor, fashion editor, and creative director for *Vogue, Allure,* and *Harper's Bazaar.* She has herself reached the status of fashion icon, and knows it: "I call myself the oldest living sittings editor." She is also the industry's Madonna, known only by her first name.

Her imprimatur on a fashion photograph is distinctive—what she calls "voyeuristic and provocative." On a *W* photo shoot, for instance, she might travel to a place such as San Salvador to scout locations. "We start with the concept of a house, stones, and steps," she says. "When the shooting starts, there has to be total concentration. I need my space to create the mood and the ambience." Mellen works in a stream-of-consciousness narrative with a conspiratorial edge. "I follow the camera. If the camera's moving, I move with it. If the photographer's running, I run behind him. It doesn't matter what he's doing—I'm doing it too," she says. Mellen strikes a compelling chord because of her hands-on approach and connection to the crucial moment of the shutter's click.

It is difficult to reconcile her patrician elegance with the person some have called the most daring and erotic of fashion's super-editors. She likes to project the feeling of sexuality caught off-guard; the viewer is an active participant in many of her open-ended editorials.

When the legendary Diana Vreeland joined *Vogue* in the mid-1960s, she hired Richard Avedon and Polly Allen Mellen. Mellen was perhaps the first editor to take photo shoots out of the studio and into exotic climes. Now, such remote location shoots are standard procedure, yet Mellen remains a master at bringing the sensually exotic into styling. A staunch individualist, Mellen knows that she is responsible for the sexually charged sensibilities of her subjects: "You can tell when you're being given the chance to let go."

Superstar Stylist **Polly Allen Mellen**

"I need my space
to create the mood
and the ambience."

Wendy Schecter was, by her own account, a Barbie-fixated child. As an adult, she has transformed that love of dress-up into a career dressing real people. Her clients include Andie McDowell, Angelina Jolie, Anne Heche, Arnold Schwarzenegger, and Annette Bening—and that's just the A list. She is the stylist to know if designers want to see their clothes at the Academy Awards and in magazines such as *Vanity Fair, Interview, Allure,* and *Bikini.*

Schecter likes to collaborate with her clients. "Things work best for me if they are organic and flow naturally," she explains. "I work with a lot of people as a natural progression from friendship or as an assignment that blossoms into something more." Of Drew Barrymore, she comments, "We were friends before we worked together, and styling her never feels like work. It's like having the best Barbie doll." The first feature film she worked on was *Skipped Parts,* with Barrymore and Jennifer Jason Leigh. Although she was originally hired to work solely on Barrymore's wardrobe, Schecter quickly became the film's wardrobe mistress.

"What did you do?" is the highest compliment anyone can pay Schecter. She explains, "I make my clients look like themselves. I take the kernel of their style and make it shine." Style, in Schecter's estimation, is more enduring than fashion: "My clients are too busy reading scripts, doing voice-overs and blockings, and rehearsing to find the clothes that will help them be the people they know they are and want others to see. I want to do that for them. It's easy for me."

"I make my clients look like themselves."

Wendy Schecter

Stylist for Celebrities and Models

Debra

"Television is fashion's superhighway."

Known for her undying energy, Debra McGuire designs costumes that are featured prominently on several hit television shows, including "Friends." She has almost achieved the celebrity status of the stars she costumes. McGuire is a regular shopper at Los Angeles stores such as Fred Segal, Neiman Marcus, and the L.A. Apparel Mart. She also frequents designer resale shops and swap meets and works directly with local designers. With these resources, she personally creates the bulk of the costumes for many of the characters on her roster of shows. Of the exhilarating pace of media style, McGuire notes, "Regular designers have to endure several months lead time. Television is fashion's superhighway."

She recalls the hectic early days of "Friends": "I created everything—it was a big job. We got a script on Monday, and we would shoot on

McGuire

Friday. There were six main characters and three guest stars per episode. I was doing about a hundred garments per week." Now, she has five assistants on each of her shows, but she is less manager than auteur. Currently McGuire is one of America's most in demand costume designers, and an ever-growing number of television producers seek her out. She aspires to be a worthy heir to the tradition of Hollywood legend Edith Head.

Arianne Phillips

Music and Makeover Stylist

This star of film and music videos is not a rock 'n' roller or an actress but rather a powerful behind-the-scenes force. New York–born, Los Angeles–based Arianne Phillips brings an East/West sensibility to her work as a stylist, wardrobe mistress, and costume designer. With a recommendation from Robert Tuner, the

Flynt. That film introduced Phillips to Courtney Love, and she built a relationship with the actress/musician, influencing Love's miraculous grunge-to-glamour makeover. Soon, Love was on the cover of *Vogue* and other magazines. Love in turn introduced Phillips to Madonna, whom she dressed in neo-Goth

"I'm much more into fantasy than realism."

former creative director of *Vogue*, Phillips began by styling for major fashion photographers but soon parlayed her love of music into projects for record companies from Warner Brothers to Elektra. Her breakthrough was the result of work with the then unknown Lenny Kravitz. "He was putting his first record together, and we created a look for him. Like Madonna, he reinvents himself all the time," Phillips comments. Her credit on the Kravitz album boosted her visibility, and soon she was working on feature films, such as *The People vs. Larry*

Oliver Thysskens for the Academy Awards and styled for the covers of *Harper's Bazaar* and *Rolling Stone*.

Most costume designers are not stylists, and vice versa, but the combination is a perfect fusion for Phillips: "As a photo stylist, you're totally dependent on what the designers create. I'm much more into fantasy than realism. Often you design the principal characters and then you shop the rest, or thrift it, or you find it at costume houses—it's a creative process in itself."

The subject of countless articles on celebrity styling, L'Wren Scott is quick to state her history: "I was six-foot-three and weighed 123 pounds, and I wanted to be a model. I worked with Bruce Weber, who advised me to leave New York. He said, 'It's not your market here—move to Paris.' I was certainly not the prevailing look."

When she arrived in Paris, she hit the jackpot: her first show was for Chanel Couture. Scott then went to work for the impresario of quirky couture, Thierry Mugler. She became his muse, wearing his weirdest ensembles; he made everything for her unique frame. Thus began her fascination with the clothes themselves.

"I was much more interested in what went on behind the scenes than in having my picture taken," she says. "I was fascinated by how much went into one picture. I was like an apprentice taking it all in."

Scott, a lover of old movies and costume designers, changed careers, shifting from modeling to styling. "I wanted to be one of the people making it happen, so I moved to Los Angeles," she says. She started working with photographers Michelle Comte and Frankie Mayer, who inspired the fledgling stylist; early tasks included trolling showrooms for clothes and taping hems on pants. On a Comte shoot with Helena Christensen, the model and Scott shopped for vintage clothing together; later that day, Christensen mentioned Scott to fashion photographer Herb Ritts.

Scott works all over the world, from styling simple photo shoots for French *Vogue* to being the creative director for the 1999 Pirelli calendar. She also worked on a *GQ* magazine cover with Sharon Stone. "The next thing I knew, I was costume-designing the remake of *Diabolique*," she says. The model turned stylist and costume designer knows her way around a camera—not only both sides of the lens but movie cameras as well.

"I was much more interested in what went on behind the scenes than in having my picture taken." —L'Wren

L'Wren

Scott

Stylist for some of the music world's biggest stars, the peripatetic Derek Khan has been instrumental in forging a connection between musicians and fashion. A native of Trinidad—where he sported red platform shoes with his Catholic high school uniform—he became a technician for one of the island's television stations and developed expertise in lighting and camera work. A big break was becoming the talent manager for the dancers who taught Madonna how to vogue. "Those guys got me to a level where I had never been," says Khan. Another stroke of luck was a meeting with a record executive who flew him to Los Angeles to outfit Salt-N-Pepa for the 1994 Grammy Awards. He dressed them in Chanel. "This was the first time Chanel had been associated with this type of music," he recalls. "Following that, I wrapped Mary J. Blige in Saint-Laurent and Dolce & Gabbana." Choosing both clothing and decor, Khan has worked for Blige, Queen Latifah, Jennifer Lopez, and others on albums, magazine covers, tours, and videos.

The 1999 "Rock" exhibition at the Metropolitan Museum of Art's Costume Institute in New York highlighted the influence on fashion of contemporary music and performers' costumes. Most surprising for Khan was that his styling was prominently featured. He recalls, "I got a call from Stephen Cirona at Tommy Hilfiger, followed quickly by a note from Myra Walker and Philippe de Montebello who chose most of Madonna's Dolce & Gabbana collection." The exhibition displayed not just what Madonna wore on tour but the breadth of Khan's diverse styling career. "Who would have thought that my work would be in the museum?" he marvels.

"I can't imagine why couture was not worn by these stars before," says Khan. "Nobody ever would have thought that hip-hop would have evolved into what it is. There is an undeniable evolution of music, and with it comes style. We've reached the moment when fashion is music and music is fashion. We are in a time when there is a real fusion of style."

Derek Khan

Rap's Star Stylist

"We've reached the moment when fashion is music and music is fashion."

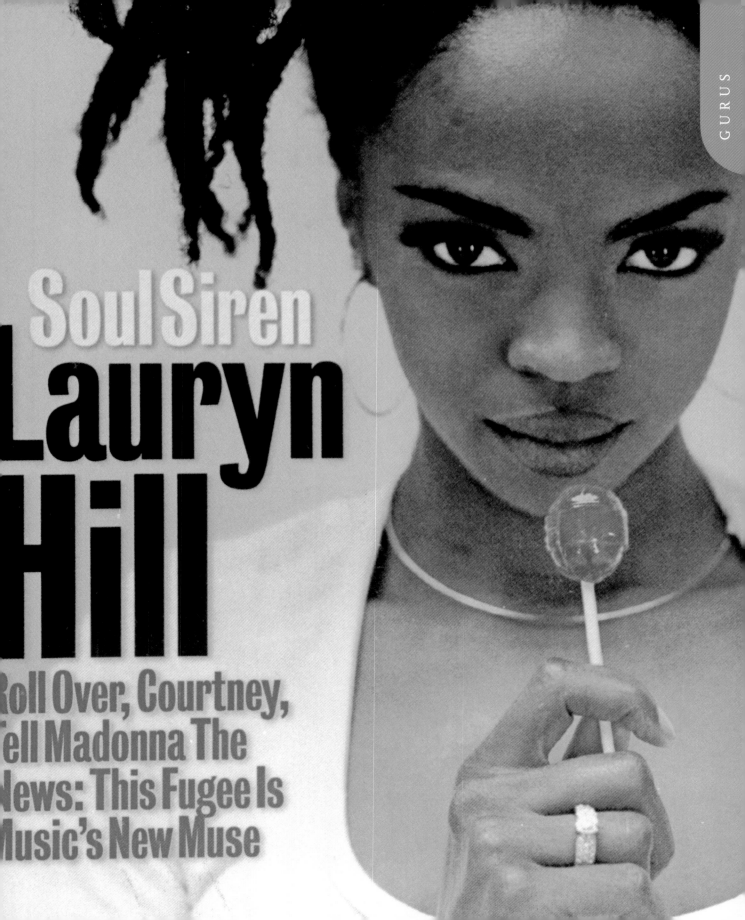

Soul Siren
Lauryn Hill

Roll Over, Courtney, Tell Madonna The News: This Fugee Is Music's New Muse

The Communicators: Talking the Talk

In fashion, the medium dictates the message. For the designer, the message of each season's look is disseminated by a public-relations professional. The services of Paul Wilmot, Ian MacKintosh, or Rados Protic can cost more than a season's worth of fabrics. The fashion team of every retail store is besieged weekly by hundreds of designers and the firms they engage. Each store's fashion director, in turn, must translate the designers' messages into the store's idiom, as Arlene Goldstein does for Saks Fifth Avenue, using newsletters, videoconferencing, and even trend analysis in order to influence how and for whom the buyers buy. The ultimate message is tailored for the consumer: from the newest category of television fashion reportage with flamboyant personalities like Leon Hall to savvy fashion writers in every region of the country.

"I have helped make the general public aware that fashion is all about what works for you."

Irreverent Fashion Host

Leon Hall

It is not just Style Network's hilarious television show "Fashion Emergency" that makes guest host Leon Hall proud of his career in the industry. "I have helped make the general public aware that fashion is all about what works for you, what you feel comfortable in, and what you can afford," he notes. Hall started in the fashion world in an era when only one look was the right look, even if it did not work on every body type. He explains, "People are finally taking a ride on the train that I've been in the front of. For a long time all those cars behind me have been empty."

Hall is also the creative director of the Fashion Mart in Dallas, a gargantuan mall with dozens of showrooms for the trade only; it is where wholesale powerhouses are built. Five times a year, Hall pulls together everything from sportswear to accessories from these different showrooms in his regional trend looks. "The fashion storyboard isn't done by a stylist, it's done by me journalistically," Hall emphasizes. "What I'm saying to five thousand buyers is that these are the five key looks of the season. I'm telling major stores and small stores that if they're buying more than five or six of the trends shown on the boards or mannequins, they don't have any direction." Hall thinks that his real-world work for the Fashion Mart keeps his television show more connected to what is happening in the world of fashion: the looks that his buyers are most excited about are featured prominently on the air as well.

Paul Wilmot

In an industry crowded with youthful and inexperienced public-relations companies, Paul Wilmot's eponymous firm is a polished and professional operation, mirroring the singular style of its founder. In a serene loft in downtown Manhattan—sensuous silk curtains are used as room dividers—the thirty-five-member staff of Wilmot Communications caters to the world's dominant brands. Young employees skirt noiselessly around the periphery, rushing products to *Vanity Fair* and *Harper's Bazaar*. Bicycle messengers send out dozens of packages each day for photo shoots, music videos, and celebrity and product "style outs." Style outs determine the products used for editorial content, and "they're the whole game," Wilmot says. "Getting clients' products into print and electronic editorial is what we do. That always influences sales positively."

With his young partners, Ridgely Brode and Stormy Stokes, Wilmot gives his prestigious clients a selection of strategic services—far more than what is offered by a typical public-relations firm. That includes basic public relations as well as event planning and product launches. His clients include brands such as Cole Haan and Holland & Holland. "Image is all about lifestyle and everyone wanting to have great quality, which could be the luxury of $110 jeans, not just $1,200 Gucci jeans or a $20,000 bracelet," Wilmot says. "People are about whatever it is that is the best product. My clients are already there—they understand."

The trajectory of one of his high-caliber clients, Thomas Pink, is an example of his global thinking about market positioning, brand building, and public-relations strategies in a fast-changing market: "They don't sell wholesale. They opened up in the late 1990s in the United States, and now the Madison Avenue store alone rings up sales of $10 million a year." Bottom-line driven Wilmot Communications helped create this phenomenon. "Thomas Pink has a point of view and well-designed, superior quality," states Wilmot. The exclusivity of the label and the firm's relationships with editors come together in what Wilmot calls a "harmonic convergence." "When you have the perfect product and aggressive people who are honest and diligent in promoting the product, you can get a lot of newspaper, television, and magazine press reaching critical mass about eight months after a launch," he posits. The usually decorous Wilmot grins as he describes the "feeding frenzy" after *GQ* magazine ran an editorial showing a stack of Thomas Pink shirts in outrageous colors: "People were calling in and ordering the stack—the whole stack."

"Image
is all
about
lifestyle
and
everyone
wanting
to have
great
quality."

Ian Mac

"I want my designers to be stars sans the unnecessary drama of the pre-show chaos."

Kintosh

After a brief stint as an intern for the Council of Fashion Designers of America—which turned into a three-year odyssey assisting executive director Fern Mallis—Ian MacKintosh was hooked on the drama of fashion. It was a whirlwind experience for the young fashion student: "The CFDA was just starting the tents plus doing the landmark benefit Seventh on Sale in San Francisco for AIDS and the CFDA awards gala. It was a time of energy, excitement, and exhaustion."

MacKintosh then worked briefly for Eva Chun and Marc Jacobs at Perry Ellis, where he learned the inner workings of fashion public relations. He explains, "The up side of working in-house is being able to concentrate on one product, one image, one identity." Many public-relations aspirants, he notes, work for outside firms with the hope of eventually working in-house, a life full of perks and times of relative peace.

Still, MacKintosh chose a different route. He could not pass up the opportunity to work with legendary publicist Eleanor Lambert. The ninety-five-year-old doyenne of American public relations, the founder of the CFDA, the Coty Awards, and the international best-dressed list, Lambert involved MacKintosh in every aspect of her business. The six-year stint gave him an unparalleled view of American fashion at its zenith, working with fashion icons such as Bill Blass and Oscar de la Renta. MacKintosh also learned the perils and pitfalls of owning a public-relations company in the often fickle world of fashion designers and their even more fickle financial backers. But he was smitten: "It definitely inspired me to start my own company. Working for someone as revered as Eleanor I had been taught by a master and knew the intricacies of the business."

Today he and Diana Wright are partners in Iliad Communications and Production. He describes the firm's range of services: "We do everything from special events to graphic design, web design, speech writing, and runway production down to the nitty-gritty of product placement." MacKintosh is known for unceasing work on behalf of his clients—trailing camera crews into shows and showrooms alike, devising charity promotions and celebrity tie-ins. Gone are the days when a fashion show alone guaranteed preeminence in the fashion press. He comments, "Today you have to consider celebrity dressing, award shows, corporate sponsorship, and promotions—e-tailing as well as retailing—and now there are hundreds of magazines and television shows to be pitched. After a grueling ten-day fashion 'week,' I want my designers to be stars sans the unnecessary drama of the pre-show chaos that prevails in this industry."

Rados Protic

Publicist for European Talent

A former editor at German *Vogue,* Rados Protic had a premonition in the 1980s that the United States would provide the fashion of the next decade. She was one of the first European editors to migrate west. "At the time I came here, New York was considered something of a backwater fashion-wise," recollects Protic. "Today, it's the center of the business and marketing side. Everything comes together here." The accuracy of her analysis is evident in the number of American designers at the helm of European labels such as Gucci, Celine, Louis Vuitton, and Yves Saint-Laurent.

"America is the center of global information and media, and that includes fashion," she states. Protic navigates the complex business, advertising, public-relations, and sales aspects of a fashion house for clients including huge European brand Bogner and the designer label Sonia Bogner and also smaller clients such as Marlies Moeller and Udi Behr. She has stretched her role beyond public-relations basics: "I try to position my clients in the U.S. market, and that means with the media and distribution channels. I tell them the right channels for their brands—from department stores to specialty stores and the Internet." Each company requires a specific venue in the fractured, multilayered consumer market.

Protic concentrates on marketing her clients: "Marketing is not merely selling, finding distribution channels such as retail, wholesale, e-tail, or licensing. It's building brand identity—establishing brand integrity in the product lines—from the store designs down to the packaging. It's using both strategic public relations and advertising to target the right customer." She understands the complexities and methodologies of the international fashion trade. For instance, many European designers open small boutiques to do their own selling; Americans love department stores, and for decades American designers did not open their own boutiques. This trend has changed in the United States, notably on Madison Avenue and in midtown and Soho in New York.

Protic was also years ahead of the fashion pack in predicting that celebrities would supplant supermodels on the covers of fashion magazines. Isabella Rossellini, Raquel Welch, and Brooke Shields are among the stars she proposed for German *Vogue* during her stewardship there, and she still uses celebrity placement as part of her core strategy. As a European in the United States, Protic sees the world of fashion from a global vantage point.

> "America is the center of global information and media, and that includes fashion."

All the newest color and trend information cannot find its way onto a store rack without the retail instinct of a store fashion director. Saks Incorporated's Arlene Goldstein has the instincts of a safari hunter—her hunting grounds are the trendiest sections of London, Milan, and Paris, where she snares the looks her customers will want. She travels to showrooms, fabric shows, and runway shows in every fashion capital several times a year to translate designers' messages for her store buyers.

Goldstein's job evolved from both the special events/public-relations work she did for more than a decade and her job as fashion director of Parisian, the dominant southeastern and midwestern retail chain acquired by Proffitts in the mid-1990s. In July 1998, Proffitts bought the world-famous Saks Fifth Avenue department-store chain; the company then morphed into Saks Incorporated. Goldstein services the 237 branches of this 70-city department-store chain. Every trend she touts affects the enormous annual sales volume of the stores and directly shapes Saks's private label program. From her front-row seat at the top fashion shows, Goldstein determines how to interpret the key looks for Saks's vast, far-flung, and diverse fashion empire. "We're one voice when it comes to private brands, whether it be accessories, young men's, or better sportswear," she states. Her observations run from the specific—"cropped pants are it"—to the strategic. "Several years ago, I was shopping in Bon Marché in Paris," she recalls. "I felt overwhelmed by the amount of floor space devoted to wraps and shawls. That's when I made the push for us to develop a similar approach."

Goldstein communicates with Saks store buyers constantly through intramedia outlets such as videoconferencing. When she goes on fashion-hunting expeditions in places such as Saint-Tropez, Barcelona, and Amsterdam, she promotes her finds on "The Fashion Buzz" on Saks TV. She also contributes to an award-winning internal newsletter, with columns called "Ask Arlene" and "What's Hot Now." Goldstein describes her role as a fashion finder and translator who is always attempting to connect what she sees on the runways with the clientele of Saks stores. "I don't take things at face value. We have our own filter, our Saks viewpoint, as well as unique perspectives by region and store," she remarks. "I'm also in the business of creating obsolescence. I want people to come into our stores and redo their wardrobes."

Arlene Goldstein

Department Store's Fashion Voice

WHAT'S HOT NOW

The Style is in the Details
Prep Your Summer Wardrobe with Hot Must-Haves

Arlene Goldstein, Fashion Director for Saks Incorporated, can answer your toughest fashion questions. Send email to arlene-goldstein@saksinc.com or fax to 205-940-4242. Catch "Fashion Buzz" on Saks TV.

Spring 2000 is an ode to femininity – printed capris, romantic florals, sexy shawls wearable chic from one-of-a-kind looking accessories to barely there basics.

Getting your warm weather wardrobe in shape for the season will be a cinch when you choose from the following trend-right items. Get ready for an instant update!

For spring 2000, you need these pieces:
1. A cropped pant
2. Anything animal
3. Bunches of bracelets
4. An embellished handbag
5. A barely there top (cami, halter or tube)
6. A knee length skirt
7. A sexy slide
8. A printed slip dress
9. A fitted shirt
10. A fringed wrap

And for the gentlemen, effortless weekend wear options go beyond casual work days. Seek:
• Tropical print camp shirts
• Flat front twill pants
• Novelty dress-casual shirts in microfiber
• Tees (for layering)
• Euro comfort sandals or slides. ■

Be daring – mix with prints or update black pants or khakis.

Iridescent fabric.

The spring tie: a feminine peasant detail.

Walk on the wild side. zebra, snake, hair calf, pony.

Capris are perfect with a boatneck tee or fitted shirt.

New elbow length sleeve with faux cuffs.

Pale colors herald the first breath of spring.

Newest printed or trimmed.

Try ankle length capris, clam diggers, or longer Bermudas.

Perfect complement for sportswear items or a sexy summertime slip dress or tank.

Great over barely there tops and dresses.

60's Bohemian inspired.

Fitted; shaped silhouette and often with stretch for comfort.

Gloss beads or semi precious nuggets.

A great way to add color.

Jacket substitute – great with cropped pant or slim skirt.

Fringed piano shawl.

ASK ARLENE

Q: Dear Arlene, "Fashion has gotten so casual... for spring 2000, are jackets becoming obsolete?"

A: Dear Trend-Tracker,
For Y2K it's all about ease so first and foremost, clothes are lightweight. So long as jackets fill the bill...weightless – relaxed – in modern shapes, they still have a very important place in any wardrobe.

The newest jackets for men & women have less inner tailoring:
• less structure
• linings seem absolutely weightless or completely disappear
• shorter, boxy shapes & longer knee length options are newest for women.
• golf and motorcross details surface

• techno fabrics and finishes create an instant update.

Hey guys – the collapsed sportcoat is a perfect pairing for plain front khakis or slacks.

Q: Dear Arlene,
"Luxury was so much a part of the mix for fall '99; will we have to give it all up for spring 2000?"

A: Dear Reader,
Most definitely not! Many of the warm weather essentials have a luxurious side with details that offer a flair for the exotic.

Ethnic embroideries, intricate beads, diaphanous silks and fabulous fringes are everywhere.

It's a banquet – have a taste! ■

WHAT'S HOT NOW

Translating Designer Collections
From Runway to Real-Way: Adapting Fresh Looks for Living

Arlene Goldstein, Fashion Director for Saks Incorporated, can answer your toughest fashion questions. Send email to arlene-goldstein@saksinc.com or fax to 205-940-4242. Catch "Fashion Buzz" on Saks TV.

Have you flipped through the latest Vogue magazine, been stopped in your tracks by images on fashion television, and asked yourself: "Who on earth would wear THAT?" Sometimes designer creations need toning down for one to wear comfortably.

Well, what you see on the runways are, in most cases, exaggerated pieces poised to get the attention of fashion editors, retailers, and the media. Many of the items are tweaked or reinterpreted and presented in a more understandable reality, once they hit more of our stores.

Often a look that seems outrageous at first glance can take on a whole new personality when teamed with a basic from your closet. Sometimes it is a trim or a detail that's brought to the masses, not the look head to toe as first presented in the designer collections. Below are some runway styles, toned-down for you to assume with comfort and style. ■

ASK ARLENE

Q: Dear Arlene,
I keep hearing the term "Utility Chic." What exactly does it mean?

A: Dear Reader,
Utility Chic is a general term for clothing with details, trims, and materials that are borrowed from performance gear. Uniforms, extreme sports, and sports equipment lend inspiration to casual sportswear. Elements such as pocket zips, webbing mesh, nylon, bungee cords, snaps, velcro, and more have made fashion news.

"Sport Chic" isn't going away altogether, but elements like zips, cargo pockets, and hoods are becoming less obvious and definitely more refined. ■

A Color Comeback for Spring 2000	Tunic Length Tops	Embroidered Tops, Skirts, and Accessories	Gingham Pattern Returns	A Sexy Slip Dress

• Color head to toe returns.
• Color played against white looks fresh.

• Here's our interpretation from our private brands.
• Perfect with a cropped pant or knee-length skirt.
• Wear it as a jacket substitute.
• Try contrasting tunic and sweater.

• Embrace an eclectic mix.
• Play it against less busy options.
• A great way to add color and texture.

• It's part of the skirt alerts for Spring 2000.
• Easy for manufacturers at every price-point to interpret.
• The printed print goes to all lengths – knee with a spaghetti strap with ¾ length sleeves.

• Newest in sheer fabrics.
• Try with floral patterns or ruffle trim.
• Wear a barely there sandal or slide.

> "We have our own filter, our Saks viewpoint, as well as unique perspectives by region and store."

The Out-of-Towners

Regional journalists travel the world attending every manner of fashion show and spectacle, distilling the spectrum of fashion prophecies and tailoring them to local audiences. The importance of such journalists' work has recently garnered recognition in the form of a coveted CFDA Fashion Award.

Atlanta and its paper of record, the *Atlanta Journal-Constitution,* stand at the crossroads of the Old South, with its genteel charm, and the New South, with its diversity and zest for the modern. The newspaper's lifestyle editors, Marylin Johnson and A. Scott Walton, embody these twin elements of southern regional fashion journalism. Readers learn how shows were staged in the early days of the New York fashion scene: "The shows were held at the Delmonico, where we would actually be seated at tables, and the designers—Pauline Trigère, Oscar de la Renta, Bill Blass, and Geoffrey Beene—were always available for a chat," says Johnson. In the current era of giant catwalks and stadium-size fashion extravaganzas, it is more challenging for regional editors to get a good look. Johnson and Walter make frequent forays to international fashion hot spots, bringing the cutting-edge looks back home season after season.

Chris Bynum, fashion reporter for the New Orleans *Times-Picayune,* regularly covers the international designers who visit New Orleans each year, but her true passion is seeking out homegrown talent. The dynamic city provides a great deal of raw material for this fifteen-year veteran of fashion journalism, from outlandish Mardi Gras costumes to the macabre fascination with burial outfits. Simultaneously, she condenses the vast amount of fashion information from national and international designers into what works in the particular climate of New Orleans. Summer wools, for example, have no place in the muggy and hot city. But she finds an eager audience for the most extreme trends that designers tout. Says Bynum, "People may think of New Orleans as provincial, but I think of it as avant-garde with all the writers, painters, and poets gravitating here to be creative."

The top fashion journalist in the Midwest, Lisa Lenoir of the *Chicago Sun-Times,* looks at fashion, and particularly fashion journalism, as a conduit to social, political, and economic issues. She aims her coverage at the ever wider audience for fashion, especially street fashion. Lenoir also makes it her mission to ferret out local talent. Mindful that Halston had his breakthrough as a result of a *Sun-Times* journalist years ago, Lenoir stays closest to those undiscovered. She comments, "My job is part visionary, part trend-setter, and part provider of information."

**Marylin Johnson
and A. Scott Walton**

Chris Bynum

Lisa Lenoir

121

The Shutterbugs: Capturing the Visual Message

Early issues of *Vogue* and *Town & Country* were heavily illustrated with quaint renderings that speak of a bygone era; today, photography has become the visual medium of the magazine publishing industry. A photograph captures everything: photo reportage shows fashion and style minute by minute; art photography presents the fundamental aesthetic shifts of fashion evolution over the long term.

Certain photographers—Patrick McMullan, who covers the party scene nonstop, or Gerardo Somoza and Mary Hilliard, who cluster around the ends of runways—chronicle the daily moments of quotidian glamour. The hard-edged advertising images of Dah Len and the avant-garde views of Hassan Jarane represent art photography—visual statements that capture the fashion zeitgeist. Kelly Klein has followed a different path, part fashion journalism, part book projects. In all cases, the photographic image of a designer's work is as critical as the designer's initial sketch.

Patrick McMullan

The prolific celebrity photographer Patrick McMullan attended business school at New York University but forsook corporate culture for nocturnal prowling. "While I was an undergraduate, I was working for a photographer and really loved it," he recalls. McMullan covered the parties for Annie Flanders at *Details:* "It was really a late-night thing: sleeping all day and people still at their offices at 11 p.m." He notes that midnight is his noon.

McMullan quickly began to freelance for *Taxi* and *Interview.* "Then I met Fern Mallis, who really liked my work and gave me a pass, and I started to cover parties for the Council of Fashion Designers of America," he comments. "Not long after, I began working for *Harper's Bazaar.*" He had plunged into the heart of the fashion world.

But then he hurt his jaw: "I wound up in the hospital for five days and couldn't cover the parties. My nephew had been assisting me for a while, and my clients were really understanding and let him do the work." Thus was born what he describes as the House of McMullan; today he hosts segments of "Full Frontal Fashion" on the Metro Channel and employs six assistants. "They have to work not only in my photographic style but in my style as a professional: they have to be polite and not too pushy—but pushy enough to get the picture. It's a delicate balance," he says. "The celebrities are incidental, a necessary evil. What I really like to do is take pictures of everyone at the party. I'm really more of a bar mitzvah photographer."

"**What I really like to do is take pictures of everyone at the party.**"

She embodies the marriage of image and fashion.

After two decades in the industry working for, and then married to (but now divorced from), designer Calvin Klein, Kelly Klein segued into a career in fashion photography. "I've always taken pictures and collected photography," Klein says of her transition from buying works by Richard Avedon and Irving Penn to modeling her work career after them. Her first clients had to trust that her eye was as blue-chip as her surname: "People considered me to be a designer. So I had to prove myself. My pictures had to be little bit better. In many ways, my name has been a hindrance."

She embodies the marriage of image and fashion. A turning point for Klein came with the publication of *Pools* in 1992, one of the first theme-photography books to tap into the huge market for popular interior design books. Her latest book, *Cross*, published in October 2000, attempts to reach the same audience. Klein currently has an active schedule of editorial shoots for French and British *Vogue,* Italian *Marie-Claire,* and *Jane,* along with advertising shoots for several big industry brands. "Beautiful photography can be boring," states Klein. She strives to ensure that hers is not.

Photographer of
Fashion and Interiors

Kelly
Klein

In the somewhat desolate yet ultra-fashionable streets of Manhattan's meatpacking district, Dah Len has transformed an old factory into a coolly appealing studio. Within this live-work environment, Len, an architect turned musician and fashion photographer, has brought together banks of camera equipment and his collection of exceptional

The cosseted son of a Hong Kong industrialist father with vast chemical holdings and an acclaimed songstress mother legendary for her beauty, Len says of his childhood in British-ruled Hong Kong, "I was brought up in privilege—beauty everywhere." Yet he rejected this life and threw himself into the punk world. In New York's Alphabet City,

The turning point in his career was his early editorial work for *Mademoiselle;* his notoriously erotic Guess? campaign is a professional landmark. He also photographed Madonna, an intractable perfectionist; Len had first to cajole and then to command her to grant him free rein. "There were portfolios everywhere from all the really great

He transformed fashion photography with a style that combines riotous color and oblique angles.

twentieth-century modular furniture. Red vinyl boxes and Mongolian lamb throws keep his two shar-peis company. He has a neo-Buddhist altar, and his latest soundtrack, haunting and soulful, plays in the background.

his neighbors included rocker Billy Idol and the record industry executive who produced Len's first compact disk. However, it was a world of drugs and empty partying; to escape he returned to photography, the art of his youth. Although he had no formal training, he transformed fashion photography with a style that combines riotous color and oblique angles. His haunting, unlikely couplings scintillate the eye.

photographers, the geniuses, the famous ones, and there I was with my camera ready to shoot Madonna, this incredible star, this world beauty," he recalls, smiling at his good fortune.

Art and Fashion Imagemaker **Dah**

Len

With protective agent Rona Siegel always by his side, Hassan Jarane is navigating the treacherous waters of fashion photography. Siegel is a fierce advocate for new talent such as Jarane; while fashion photography claims to be a barometer of change, it often clings to a stable of celebrity photographers who are sometimes as famous as the models and movie stars they photograph. It takes a Rona Siegel to break the viselike grip.

Jarane shoots for *Vibe, Paper,* and *Allure,* as well as big-name design

Hassan

companies. Like most photographers, he relies on advertising shoots rather than editorial ones to pay the bills. "Advertising is still important for real money," says Jarane. "Fortunately clients like Nike and Sony are exciting. I'm lucky."

Jarane believes he brings the characteristics of film to the world of fashion photography. Creating the feeling of something moving in a picture is an ability that comes from his experience as a filmmaker in Morocco. "Right now, photographers are copying one another," says Jarane. "It's sad because they all look like one another, and even the young photographers are copying the ones imme-

diately preceding them. There is a fear of being imaginative, but there needs to be an intellectual challenge. Talented art directors believe in the vision I have."

He constantly analyzes his chosen field: "It's important to know how people look at a picture. You have to be arrested by the visual—it needs to stop you. It's all about the image and the vision. You need to get excited or you're dead." Jarane continues, "The best photography is collaborative, and as a filmmaker, I bring that to my work."

Jarane's photographs, which can look like the result of intense computer manipulation, are actually pure camera work. He notes that still photography evolves in response to new technology, particularly the Internet and three-dimensional imaging, but thinks that technology has its limits. "The photographer will never be obsolete," says Jarane. "No matter what technology you have in front of you, you're not going to get the shot without the photographer's eye—it's all about personal vision."

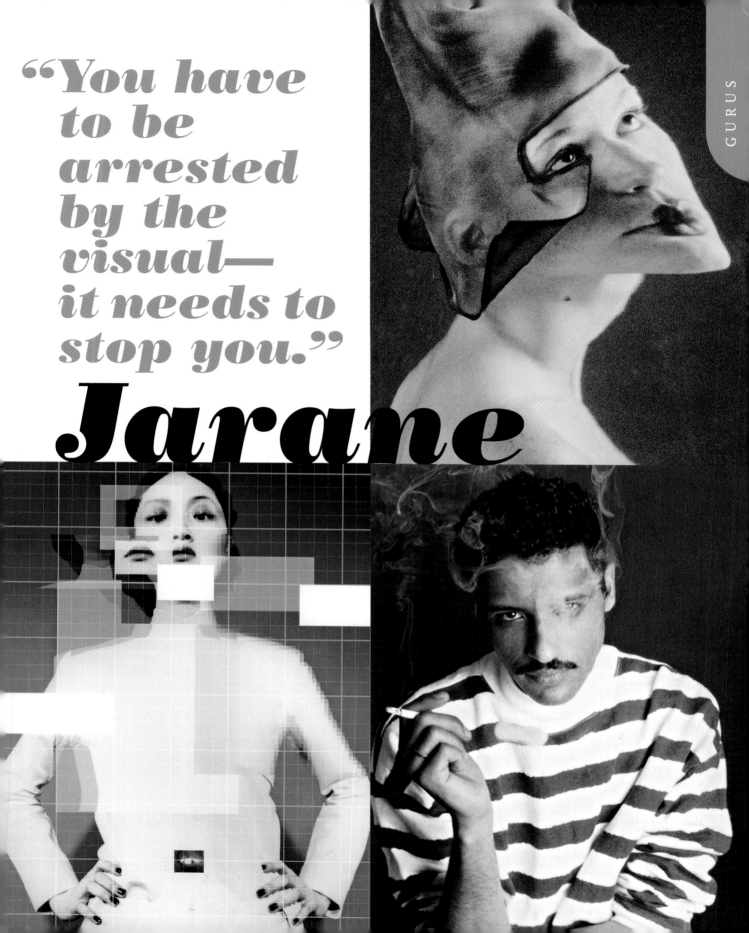

"You have to be arrested by the visual— it needs to stop you."

Jarane

"I'm at the shows covering fashionable people, not really the runway."

Mary Hilliard

Fashion's Behind-the-Scenes Photographer

One lone woman often takes a position in the pack of male paparazzi: Mary Hilliard. Rejecting the apparatus of traditional photography—studio lighting and styling, repetitive product shots—she has concentrated on the reporting side of fashion, seeking the human stories behind the glitter and glamour.

Life magazine editor Sally Kirkland first introduced Hilliard to designers Bill Blass, Geoffrey Beene, and Oscar de la Renta, as well as premier fashion journalist Carrie Donovan. "I started going to fashion shows, and André Leon Talley and Billy Norwich helped me, too," she recalls. "I like the intersection of the social and fashion worlds, and these designers and editors are why I'm successful." She has a contract with *Vogue* and works for other publications as well; for Vogue.com she now shoots digital.

At the shows for the New York and Paris collections, she is as interested in the audience as the models. "I'm at the shows covering fashionable people, not really the runway. I'm in the audience as they arrive, capturing the fashion, the celebrities, and the atmosphere," she says.

Gerardo Somoza

**Fashion's
Sharpshooter**

Gerardo Somoza has covered many fashion shows from the frenzied photographers' pit at the end of the runway. Today, he states, "I will only get down there for Donna Karan." He prefers studio and magazine work. On the set he is an island of calm in a feverish sea of assistants, stylists, models, hair and makeup people, and art directors. Somoza quietly moves around and through the tumult, sidestepping the designer and the league of helpers to do the styling himself. His is the fashion photography that sells fashion, and his client list starts with *Allure*, *Details*, *GQ*, *Us* and keeps on going.

For the most part, Somoza avoids the paparazzi-filled party circuit, but on occasion he still enjoys the flashbulbs and haughty celebrities: "I still do the parties, but I have to have an assignment and good access. The same with the runway.

I like the backstage. I also love advertising and editorial." He is currently working on an exhibition devoted to both his backstage photographs and the images of models he has captured in their private moments; his work leaves no doubt that it is the calm and collected Somoza who always gets the shot.

His is the fashion photography that sells fashion.

The Backstagers: Making It Happen

The stage of fashion commands more money per minute than any other live performance. A runway presentation, typically ten minutes long, requires an astounding array of professionals: hair and makeup artists, lighting designers, deejays, producers, and more. Fashion-show producer Kevin Krier is known for his keen attention to every detail of a presentation. Jewelry designer Donatella Pellini and body-art creator Melodie Weir represent two of the fields essential to the success of a show. For the runway show is fashion as spectacle, and a designer's career hangs in the balance.

She picks up her brush and creates art that just happens to be on the skin.

In the 1960s, the model Veruschka painted herself trompe l'oeil style to match walls and windows; suddenly, makeup crossed the boundary into body art. Melodie Weir straddles the same border today. She spent the 1990s promulgating—and practicing—body art throughout the fashion world. Weir is not a cosmetician making new shades of lipstick—alongside traditional makeup teams she picks up her brush and creates art that just happens to be on the skin.

Body art has enjoyed recent favor on fashion runways. "Jean-Paul Gaultier was the first one to approach makeup as art," Weir notes. In January 1999, she flew to Paris to do the haute couture body art for designer Thierry Mugler. Mugler used as inspiration the Maori from New Zealand. "Thierry asked me to collaborate on a show that was theater," recalls Weir. "I did tribal body painting based on the Masai in chalk and also taking stuff from the Maui for faces." She claims that her art links the fashion world to anthropology and spiritualism.

Such a link was evident in her work with Donna Karan on a group of outfits to celebrate the opening night of "Body Art: Marks of Identity" at the Museum of Natural History in New York in fall 1999. Karan created the clothing and Weir the tribal faces. In 1998 Maybelline hired Weir for the Cosmic Edge campaign, which showed four different shades of henna in miniature pots. Calvin Klein underwear commissioned a group of hennaed briefs, and Weir has even camouflaged nails and cheeks for the U.S. Army. She made a foray into the wholesale end of the fashion business with a tiny space called Chant. Her front door is adorned with a fifteenth-century Buddhist temple ornament: "I started the showroom as a sacred place. It's a healing place."

Considering the future of fashion, Weir speculates, "People do not want to live in an austere, sterile environment." She predicts a rebellion against minimalism: "People want to surround themselves with comfort and color."

Outrageous Runway
Makeup Artist

Melodie Weir

> **"Accessories are made more of a protagonist than the clothing."**

Donatella

Runway Accessorizer

When one of Rome's premier fashion houses, Fendi, first sought to accessorize its runway shows in the early 1980s, its then designer, Karl Lagerfeld, turned to the Pellini family, one of Europe's best-known costume-jewelry makers. "My grandmother started this business, and my mother continued it," says Donatella Pellini, currently in charge of the Milan-based company. She has overseen the business's entry into retail and onto the runway; she is also known for her own designs.

For years, Pellini made jewelry models for Fendi shows under the direction of Gilles DuFour, Lagerfeld's close collaborator. One year, Lagerfeld told DuFour and Pellini that pasta was his inspiration for that season's Fendi collection; Pellini made three-dimensional prototypes of macaroni, penne, farfalle, and other types of pasta. Soon, a procession of pastas could be seen on everything Fendi, even leather goods. "We did it in colored resin and metals. These elements were a big success," recalls Pellini of the many hundreds of pieces produced in her family's workshop. It was Pellini's work on Lagerfeld's original food-inspired collection that may have started the company, moribund at the time, on its stunning turnaround. "Accessories are made more of a protagonist than the clothing," claims Pellini. The synthesis of all the visual elements makes for great runway style.

Pellini

"*My job is to make the designers' work shine, to convey their message.*" **Kevin**

Krier

Catwalk Mastermind

The typical fashion show is an extravaganza of glamour with quarter-mile-long runways, audiences of more than five hundred tightly packed celebrities and fashion bigwigs, and dozens of photographers jockeying for position. It takes a strong producer to oversee the hundreds of supporting players in this one-time-only performance; Kevin Krier is one of the few to have developed the necessary skills. "The cast, the music, the creation of a narrative—all these are components of the theater. I liken what I do to the work of a director. The role of playwright is that of the designer," he comments. His task is complex, exacerbated by the temperamental cast. Nevertheless, he says, "My job is to make the designers' work shine, to convey their message."

Each show is adapted to a designer's personality and budget. "You start by meeting with the designer and talking it out creatively," Krier explains. "What is the message of the season? What are the clothes telling you? How do we make this modern or how do we make that realistic? In what medium do we work? Is it about a hall that is unfinished and the models are choreographed or a theatrical proscenium opening and a traditional runway? We have to decide the best method to convey the message." There is no end to differences between designers: "They are always fun and have their own wit. Giorgio Armani is about distancing—beautiful space and beautiful clothes."

Krier is involved in every aspect of a show. "I edit the collection with the designer and the design team or stylist. We decide what's to be shown and which model will wear what outfit, and we supervise the fittings, the tailoring, and the hair and makeup meetings. We have professional dressers who dress the models, and we build a dress card during the fittings—which designers keep for their trunk shows—that catalogs exactly what's on each model," he says. "We stage-manage every element. We have wonderful music and lighting people and set designers—it's a creative team, and you have to have a dialogue. However, we are ultimately responsible." That "we" represents nine full-time staffers, a number that can triple for show week. Krier and his crew can handle sixty runway shows a year; in one week they once produced fourteen.

The Hustlers: Selling the Goods

Selling fashion is part sleight of hand and part hand-holding. The wholesale salesperson, such as Michele Fix, can come off as a real performer, talking a buyer past an ungainly seam on a sample garment or firing a customer's imagination with a sprinkle of rhinestones on a swatch glued to a pencil sketch. A retail fashion director, like Susan Forehand, must justify outrageous prices with inventive displays and designer-led trunk shows. Fashion's executives must muster all of their creative merchandising talents, whether he or she owns a company, like Herb Kosterlitz of Peggy Jennings, or runs one, like Arthur Cooke of the Italian Fin. Part SpA. Extravagant window displays—Robert Rufino's Tiffany vitrines, for example—and atmospheric, evocative boutiques—such as Assaf Ziv's Zao—create an environment that encourages acquisition. Often the last representatives of fashion's vast sales machine is the individual salesperson, who simultaneously inspires trust and sets the cash registers ringing.

New York City considers itself the only important fashion mecca in the United States, but Susan Forehand, the longtime fashion and public-relations director at Saks Fifth Avenue's Atlanta branch, is out to prove them wrong. She is the conduit between designers from New York and Europe and the city's well-heeled elite, and she has succeeded in turning the city into a special-events hotspot.

It can be difficult for designers to make an impact in key cities outside of the fashion centers. So major retailers empower branch fashion directors such as Forehand to connect designers with customers through innovative event planning. Forehand's fashion happenings bring the New York and European runway aesthetic to a wide range of customers in the South. Each season, she imports top designers such as Hubert de Givenchy, Oscar de la Renta, and Mary McFadden. Saks mounts Forehand-organized minirunway shows, or trunk shows, for the designers or hosts. (The term harks back to the days when designers brought sample clothing collections to stores in heavy steamer trunks.) Trunk shows provide an opportunity for designers to take their creations on the road; Forehand ensures that these events are attended by customers who are attuned to the look of a particular designer.

A fierce ally for her clientele, Forehand might offer tailoring recommendations and selection guidance to designers. She attempts to distill runway fashions into wearable gowns that will dazzle at Atlanta's important galas. She even provides guidance about color: in the South, where the sun is hot and ostentation is often desirable, colors tend to be bold.

Forehand defends the sophistication of her southern customers. "We get it. We aren't living in Tara without electricity. Our clients are world players," she comments. "In fashion, there is a tendency to think of any city outside New York as very provincial. This is especially true of the perception of the South. Our women travel the world, run major corporations, and act as patrons of the arts in a thriving city." Forehand must constantly remind designers of this fact: "I'm an advocate for my clients. I make bringing them the world's very best my mission."

Trunk Show Impresario Susan

"In fashion, there is a tendency to think of any city outside New York as very provincial."

Forehand

Robert Rufino's childhood in New York's Chinatown—a panoply of sights and sounds—deeply influenced the display artist. "The colors of the fruits and vegetables in pushcarts—it was like what I now know of France, it was very European," he remembers. "It was visually rich. When I first went to Paris for Henri Bendel, I felt as though I was at home."

It is the world's most famous windows, those of Tiffany's in New York City, that are now his greatest passion. He oversees visual merchandising and interior design for the premier luxury purveyor. He is also a perennial favorite of the international best-dressed list: "It's about style being right for the person. Some things are my signatures. I'm not trendy. I take things that shouldn't work together and make them work—they are Rufino-ized."

"I was very fortunate to start out at a great store, Henri Bendel," says Rufino. "There will never be another store like it. I had the best teacher in life, Geraldine Stutz." He also met Robert Currie, the window display master at Bendel. Currie interviewed Rufino one morning; he was hired immediately and kept late that very night. After eleven years at Bendel, stints at *Taxi, Harper's Bazaar,* and *Elle,* and three years at the *New York Times* with Carrie Donovan, the Rufino aesthetic—an unmistakable edgy, color-suffused visual—was firmly established.

It took twelve interviews over three months before Rufino was enlisted to succeed the legendary Gene Moore at Tiffany's: "I had really big shoes to fill. Gene was an original, and he worked at Tiffany's for forty years. At Bendel, we loved the magic Gene created with his signature windows." In fact, Moore's archive—photographs of every window—is one of the store's historic treasures. Nevertheless, Rufino continued in his own style. "I had such respect for Gene Moore that I didn't want to copy him. While I know there is never really anything that is completely new, I wanted my own point of view," he says. And now Tiffany's windows have been Rufino-ized. One may feature bust forms accessorized with classic garden hats, preserved flowers, and Schlumberger jewelry. Comments Rufino, "I love photography and every window is like looking through a camera—some windows are funny, some are sensual, and some are provocative."

Tiffany's Visual Tastemaker # Robert

"Every window is like looking through a camera."

Rufino

Couture's Wholesale
Merchandiser

Michele Fix

"The challenge is to take what we see on the runway and translate that fantasy into something that is going to be commercial, wearable, and desirable."

Even the most magnificent clothes do not sell themselves. It is the task of the wholesale sales team to present the designer's vision in a way that captures the customer's imagination. Michele Fix, director of sales for Givenchy wholesale, has the daunting task of merchandising the work of the current designer, the pioneering Alexander McQueen. Fix has to make his collections look elegant rather than outré in the gilded dressing rooms of elite boutiques—avant-garde and conservative alike—around the country and around the world.

Fix operates in the real world of sizes fourteen to sixteen. "The challenge is to take what we see on the runway and translate that fantasy into something that is going to be commercial, wearable, and desirable," states Fix. Her job is to ensure that her Givenchy customers look stunning, and so she must understand style in a wide variety of cities and countries. "The department stores buy something with which they can make an overall story," Fix explains. "They try to take a relatively large representation of what is shown on the runway so they can show the essence of the collection."

Fix is sanguine about the competition and comparison shopping engendered by technology. "There are so many more venues for people to find out about fashion," she says. "There's so much more out there, with the Internet and fashion television." According to Fix, technology will have its greatest impact in the accessories realm, not on the clothes themselves: "Givenchy is a luxury firm, and we're at a high price point. Clothing is still a very tactile type of purchase."

"Peggy Jennings is the last designer selling both couture and ready-to-wear to the stores," says Herb Kosterlitz, one of the few individuals still working in American couture. The company makes money the old-fashioned way. Jennings and her son Jay create all the designs—there are no assistants, outside consultants, or focus groups—and her older son John is the factory manager.

Kosterlitz notes, "We have an advantage in being able to manufacture where other people have to rely on outside contractors. The only thing we outsource is the beading." He maintains a staff of about sixty sewers, each of whom does a garment from start to finish. "There's pride of authorship in each piece," he says of the atelier's *petits mains,* or couture sewers.

Jennings designs clothes for young women who love, and can afford, the most luxurious silks and tailoring. This type of service is not cheap. "Exquisite detail can be achieved when you are willing to pay for it," says Kosterlitz. "You're going to get both the fabric and the workmanship. It's the hand-finishing details that best describe couture. It's an individually made garment."

Kosterlitz disagrees with the notion that couture is dead: "When it's an important event, it's critical to think of how one looks. Every woman is self-conscious about something, but we make her look perfect. When a woman wears haute couture, she has the opportunity to project what she wants to project. Fashion is all about perception."

The ever-increasing desire for customization is another guarantee that a place remains for haute couture. "Individual style is more important than ever," says Kosterlitz. "The option of having changes made is what makes couture special." When a garment is made to someone's figure and not an abstract mannequin, he explains, "you can change the width of the shoulder, and add or eliminate fullness; Peggy can take any style and customize it." Couture will always live for those who feel that creating a unique personal style is worth the hefty price.

Herb

"When a woman wears
she has the
what she wants to

Kosterlitz
haute couture,
opportunity to project
project."

International Luxury-
Goods Merchant

Arthur Cooke

The creative guru for disparate corporate entities owned by Italian conglomerate Fin. Part SpA is Arthur Cooke. He oversees showrooms for sportswear company Henry Cotton's and linen company Frette, the crown jewel of the conglomerate. No hanging rack of samples is safe from his artful rearranging, no store display exempt from the cavalcade of curiosities he uses as props.

Cooke is responsible for image, merchandising, product development, store visuals, and advertising. "Our plan is to make the brands not only world leaders in their respective markets but also to make their collective images synonymous with fashion and luxury," he proclaims.

One of the industry's most famous retailers, Dawn Mello of Bergdorf Goodman, discovered Cooke. "Dawn was my mentor," he says. "This woman could single-handedly set the tone for fashion and personally decide what was good taste." In the young Cooke Mello found a disciple who would implement her credo: "The main floor sets the tone for the whole store." He explains, "If people are not turned on by the main floor, they will never go up the elevator."

At Bergdorf, Cooke started as a buyer. He picked the vendors, placed the orders, chose the accessories, and shaped the looks for the coming season. He found the hands-on aspect of the selling floor much more appealing than the spreadsheet side of retail. Cooke spent most of his time developing exclusives with designers and trolling the streets of Europe for unusual items.

The fashion world was much less sophisticated when Cooke was working his way up at Bergdorf; he would often be solicited by top editors to describe the shows he saw in Europe. "They would call me the minute I got home and say, 'Tell me, tell me!' Together, we would create trend stories," he recalls. Promoted to divisional merchandise manager with responsibility for the accessory division, he revamped the entire department. Out went traditional gold chains; in came Angela Cummings and Robert Lee Morris, launching the designer costume-jewelry phenomenon.

Within a few years, Cooke was appointed vice president of Bergdorf; he then moved to Celine, where he prepared the way for its current LVMH-led makeover. In 1999 he assumed his current position at

> ## "Our plan is to make the brands' collective images synonymous with fashion and luxury."

Henry Cotton's and Frette. Nowadays, when Cooke sees young buyers mesmerized by sell-through tables and electronic data, he commands, "Get off those computers right now—we're going to the market!"

Most of the world encounters fashion only while shopping. The shopping experience is the single indispensable fashion moment, the instant when the designer's vision must communicate itself. In the store—small boutique or enormous emporium—these messages are explicated by chicly clad sales associates.

Gone are the days of minimum wages and meager commissions. Talented in-store personnel now receive benefits, vacation packages, and impressive salaries. In a world where customers have less and less leisure time, the salesperson's role—preselecting and editing—is more critical than ever. Professionals like Alexandra Lapegna at Les Copains in New York make the buyer's life far easier. "The day of the accidental shopper and impulse buyer is gone," she states. "You have to buy for specific customers and keep meticulous records in your client book." In addition, Lapegna will go the extra mile for her clients, closing a store for a publicity-shy celebrity customer or bringing valises of garments to the hotel suite of visiting royals.

Afrodita Badescu has worked on Madison Avenue for two decades—currently at Ferragamo—and still enjoys being in the trenches of retail warfare. She treasures her relationships with some of the world's wealthiest and most watched consumers. As a teenager she worked at the legendary store Veneziano—the first designer boutique to pioneer

Versace and Ferré—and has noted a sea change in the customer and a corresponding response in the sales associates. "We are dealing not just with an affluent client but with a discerning one. It's no longer just about expensive goods, but beautiful and enduring merchandise—you might even say classics," she says. "I find that it is a tremendous challenge to make sure that we edit our collection for our customers."

Zendy Rapoport—known far and wide by only her first name—is a key salesperson for Chanel, originally in Paris as a *première vendeuse* and since the mid-1990s in New York. Her long association with the prominent house has conferred on her a type of star status usually reserved for a designer. Zendy's advice on various selections often includes an explanation of the designer's inspiration or a garment's innovative tailoring. "I listen to my customer and take in her style," she notes. "I watch what she looks at and what she touches. I am patient, and I might see something that I know will work, but it isn't until the customer tries it on that she believes."

Shoppers Personal and Otherwise

Madison

Avenue

Zendy Rapoport

Afrodita Badescu

Alexandra Lapegna

"The day of the accidental shopper and impulse buyer is gone."

Assaf Ziv

Retail Wizard

The ashram-like calm of one of New York's most outré stores, Zao, echoes the spirit of Assaf Ziv. His enterprise stands out from the pack of upstarts that has sprung up on the Lower East Side, Nolita, the meatpacking district, and Soho. For the most part, such stores, first viewed as a minirevolution in retail, have taken on a stagy, overly cool sameness, imitating Colette in Paris or 10 Corso Como in Milan. These avant-garde boutiques meld design and culture, selling fashion in a clinical environment. Zao attempts something different, and Ziv, former makeup artist and Israeli fashion editor, tracks the zeitgeist with clever interpretation rather than slavish devotion.

Zao presents cutting-edge couture, ready-to-wear, housewares, and furniture in museumlike vignettes. Scowling, snobbish salespeople are happily absent. Stories are told simply, coherently, and without condescension. Ziv wants women to shop, enjoy, take pleasure—and Zao is a visual and tactile treat.

The boutique does not try to compete with either its downtown brethren or uptown department stores. Ziv travels the world in search of emerging designers, forgotten talents, and craftspeople-artisans, many of whom are neglected in large stores that insist on immediate returns. His like-minded backers, including partner Tal Lancman, provided the freedom to create Zao. "The store is the meeting point of art and design," Ziv explains.

"The store is the meeting point of art and design."

Pla

Players

A true player, whether at the helm of a small company or a global conglomerate, is as rare as a true prophet. In fact, players are more similar to prophets than to gurus: they are often singular individuals who crave control over their staff as well as strategic freedom for their company's growth. With their marketing and business prowess, top fashion executives provide the management and business apparatus for fashion creativity and financial success.

Trade organizations have a crucial role in the business of fashion. Overseeing all of a season's fashion shows, recognizing fashion's top talents—the directors of such organizations have a place both inside and outside the industry.

Within the four walls of retail stores and wholesale showrooms, and within the virtual world of the Internet as well, the theater of presentation is essential. From a single garment to a tony boutique to an attention-grabbing web site, the art of marketing has never been more important.

The global enterprises that emerge from successful management and marketing rely on boundary-breakers in the fields of investment banking, law, and recruiting. Directing international brand names, master-minding enormous buyouts, and building flagship stores are only some of the activities that change the panorama of retail around the world.

The Organizers: Ordering the Chaos

If not for fashion's much ballyhooed professional organizations, the industry would be a fractious, undisciplined mob scene. Even despite the thoughtful governance of strong leaders such as Fern Mallis in the United States and Didier Grumbach in France, battle lines are often drawn. One designer sues another over a feminized interpretation of the classic tuxedo; yet another uses a public forum to malign a competitor. Fashion's ringleaders must rein in the personalities, marshal the press, placate the buyers, and keep the industry machine humming.

Didier

Twice a year, jumbo jets filled with American magazine editors and store buyers streak across the Atlantic Ocean; the passengers eagerly anticipate the spectacle of French fashion shows organized by Didier Grumbach. Grumbach presides over the Paris-based Fédération Française de la Couture, the largest confederacy of fashion trade organizations in the world.

The elite labels—Chanel, Givenchy, and more—sponsor shows that verge on aesthetic extravagance; for example, one season Jean-Paul Gaultier had his models walk through a watery lagoon in an industrial park on the outskirts of the city. Most of the shows, however, are held in a modern auditorium within the Louvre museum. During the shows, Grumbach can be found in the sprawling labyrinth beneath the I. M. Pei–designed Grand Louvre pyramid. In this underground bunker, Grumbach markets and schedules the biggest egos in the fashion business. He not only visits the many shows his group organizes but also serves as host extraordinaire, greeting front-row executives and guests. Grumbach also sets up a press office and oversees the communications apparatus in key fashion hotels to enable remote access to the events. "In hotel lobbies and rooms where there are internal movie systems, we provide video footage of the shows," explains Grumbach. Others receive literature and photos of the collections.

Grumbach dispels the notion that his organization benefits from national largesse. "People think that the French government pays for this. All this is private, and we have the space free, thanks to the boutiques and gift shops for tourists," Grumbach emphasizes. The Fédération's newest project belies its reputation for serving only the larger, existing houses. With hard-won support from fashion's private sector, including he all-powerful LVMH of France and GFT of Italy, the Mode & Finance fund champions fledgling European designers.

Grumbach

Grumbach markets and schedules the biggest egos in the fashion business.

Fern Mallis

Behind the monumental Beaux-Arts New York Public Library is Bryant Part, once a rundown, unsafe stretch of dirt and today the beautifully restored home of New York's fashion week. Gleaming with white tents and teeming with fashion press and buyers, the park hosts 7th on Sixth, the show whose recent sale to IMG underscores that American fashion is a global business. The event's executive director, Fern Mallis, calmly orchestrates the dozens of runway shows that are crammed into eight days.

"My goal from the beginning was to coalesce the designers as an industry," recounts Mallis of her mission on behalf of the American fashion industry. Hired by the Council of Fashion Designers of America in 1991, she has spent her time reorienting the group of American designers. "I realized that the industry was a slumbering giant," she comments. The concept of a trade organization to give American designers worldwide prestige did not come about until 1964. It was then that legendary publicist Eleanor Lambert founded the CFDA as a public-relations tool to promote American designers to national media. Lambert wrenched Bill Blass, Geoffrey Beene, and their cohorts out of their showrooms and into the limelight. But the CFDA operated as a clique of luxury designers until Mallis arrived. She recognized that the New York garment center had a neighborhood—several blocks in the thirties along Seventh Avenue—but no physical presence. Thus she developed the twice-a-year 7th on Sixth, which has helped achieve the strategic goals of the CFDA—focusing attention on American designers.

A founding board member of the Design Industries Foundation Fighting AIDS, Mallis, along with Ralph Lauren, also took the Fashion Targets Breast Cancer concept on the road to countries including Brazil and Australia, helping to create worldwide recognition of the power of American designers. During Mallis's tenure with the CFDA, many European brands have been Americanized—first Rebecca Moses in Milan at Genny, more recently Michael Kors at Celine and Marc Jacobs at Vuitton in Paris. Today, American designers are at the center of the world fashion stage, thanks in part to the successful efforts of Mallis. It is thus fitting that in summer 2001 she relinquished the reins of the CFDA to former barrister Peter Arnold.

"My goal from the beginning was to coalesce designers as an industry."

The Master Builders:
Refashioning the Fashion Landscape

As with many industries at the turn of the twenty-first century, major global consolidation has greatly affected the fashion world. Lone dressmakers in Paris, enormous billion-dollar companies: both may now have an equal effect on contemporary trends. The 1990s also gave rise to lifestyle fashion brands; marketing strategies, such as those spawned by Celine president Jean-Marc Loubier, are today calibrated for a generation of label-conscious consumers. Yves Carcelle rolls out new retail store strategies for the astonishing array of brands acquired by Moët Hennessy Louis Vuitton. Both of these men report to the fashion world's buyout king, Bernard Arnault, chairman of LVMH and without a doubt the most important businessperson in the fashion industry.

Vast retail chains take advantage of business synergies as well as hugely popular new labels. Russell Simmons, founder of Phat Farm, transforms urban music culture into a fashion house. New leadership at Italy's GFT—Roberto Jorio Fili—and New York's Bergdorf Goodman—Ronald L. Frasch—redefines luxury merchandising. Fashion's innate diversity requires much from these top merchandising strategists, who can maneuver their companies through the byzantine complexities of today's global marketplace.

The single most powerful figure in the fashion world—Bernard Arnault, chairman of the $40-billion LVMH (Moët Hennessy Louis Vuitton) Group—is disarmingly enamored of the design process: "I listen to John Galliano describe the dresses one by one, using his amazing fantasy. We go through the storyboards he has organized for the main themes of the show: scraps of fabric, a few glass beads, a beautiful vintage photograph alongside photocopied pages of magazines, a bunch of colorful feathers, some lace, and an antique silk rose. All these may be pinned on the wall of his studio. There might be a few books open to specific pages."

Arnault's fashion behemoth has sprung from his inauspicious purchase of a basket of bankrupt companies, Boussac, in 1984. One of the companies was the then down-at-the-heels fashion label Christian Dior. Arnault understood the power of the Dior label and resurrected the company's design spirit with new creative and marketing talent. He then embarked upon a rapid and revolutionary acquisition strategy that for several years has resulted in the purchase of a business a week.

Yet Arnault is extremely involved in the management of the multitudinous businesses within his fashion pyramid. His top adviser, Katell le Bourhis (responsible for the glittery Dior exhibition at the Metropolitan Museum of Art and its accompanying fête), claims that Arnault "actively participates in all the ad campaigns and all matters of importance. He has a global non-restrictive vision. He manages to run his vast empire as if it were a small company where the boss has his hands on all aspects of the business."

At the core of Arnault's empire-building strategy was the realization that synergistic brand building would net staggering monetary rewards: the sum of his labels would be worth more than the individual parts. Arnault's purchase and makeover of moribund brand Louis Vuitton was the first time he installed a maverick designer for a previously staid label. Today, with Marc Jacobs at Louis Vuitton, John Galliano at Dior, and Michael Kors at Celine, the astute businessman has fostered a climate where he works hand-in-glove with avant-garde designers.

Commentators point out that Arnault fostered the autonomy of stand-alone businesses: each company, a Savile Row shirt house like Thomas Pink or a punk-inspired cosmetics house like Hard Candy, retains its own infrastructure and identity. Indeed, LVMH leverages its marketing, manufacturing, and distribution muscle to promote smaller firms. The financial security and organizational alliance with LVMH provides countless benefits.

Arnault avers his belief in the boutique as the emblem of the designer's identity. He states, "The strongest factor in luxury brand-building is the place where you go and buy—the boutique. It is where the brand is alive in its environment, hence the importance of controlling how your products are displayed. It is also why we are not letting others create that environment for us on the Internet." An early believer in the power of cyberspace, Arnault says, "We are investing directly in e-luxury.com as we have invested and continue to invest in our network of boutiques."

The crown jewel in the LVMH network is the corporate headquarters tower in New York, designed by Christian de Portzamparc. Arnault's love for the vanguard is evident in its jutting angles and ever-pulsating light column; the building casts a new glow over the Dior boutique in its base as well as the rest of Fifty-seventh Street.

Bernard Arnault

Fashion's Foremost Empire Builder

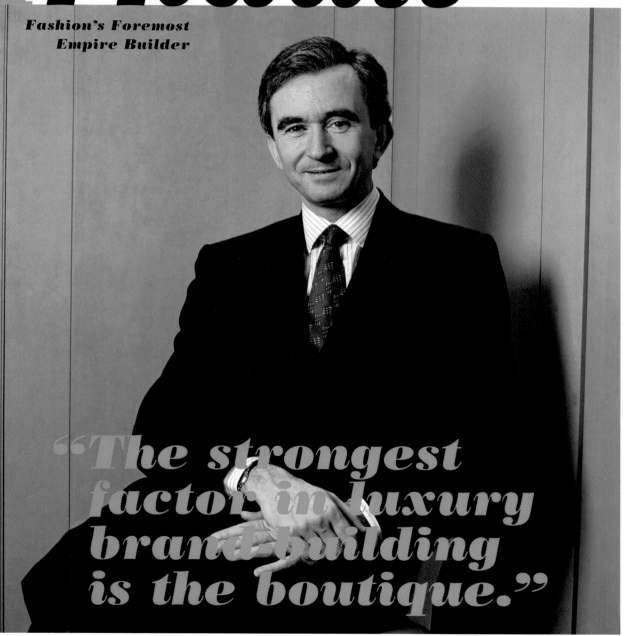

"The strongest factor in luxury brand-building is the boutique."

Ronald L.

In his first week as the chief executive officer of Bergdorf Goodman, Ronald Frasch planted himself firmly on the selling floor. He realized immediately that shoppers at Bergdorf, the world's most prestigious boutique retailer, do not shop the way that, say, Barneys customers do: "Bergdorf customers shop by floor. They say, 'I shop the third floor, I shop the fifth floor.'" To serve them better, Frasch has set out to create a new floor-within-a-store concept.

He is determined to acquaint himself with his clientele. "For the established customers, we'll do a professional focus group," says Frasch. "For the younger society group, I'm going to invite them for lunch. I don't believe in making everything impersonal—that's why I got out of retail for a while."

Frasch's desire to serve the customer is notable, given his modest retail beginnings. He recalls, "I had an aunt who worked at Bloomingdale's who said, 'Well, come on down.'" At his interview he did not know the difference between merchandising and operations. Nevertheless, he became an associate shoe buyer at Bloomingdale's. He moved to ready-to-wear at Bonwit Teller in the Kal Ruttenstein era of the mid-1970s and then to Saks Fifth Avenue, where for six years he was a divisional merchandise manager of fine apparel. Frasch joined Neiman Marcus in the mid-1980s; he developed his hands-on approach at the feet of one-time mentor Stanley Marcus, the father of luxury retailing and founder of the $2.2-billion Neiman Marcus group. As senior vice president, Frasch selected brands that would be appropriate for Neiman Marcus customers; he also banned middle-brow labels from the selling floor. He then spent four years as president of the United States division of Gruppo Finanzario Tessile, the Italian apparel consortium, and moved to Bergdorf from GFT in 2000.

"It's not about the product. It's about the entire environment," Frasch says. "The individuals we want to service want to be pleased by all their senses—no one needs to spend this kind of money. The shopping experience is emotional, it's visual, and it's tactile. You've got to be able to service all those senses. You look at the tag, and it says Bergdorf's. You bought Bergdorf's and you also bought Chanel. Most stores just sell Chanel." Bergdorf annual revenues are currently $267 million. Frasch's intensification of the retail experience underlies the elegant sophistication of the luxury establishment.

Frasch

"It's not about the product. It's about the entire environment."

The head of the ever-expanding hip-hop media and apparel empire that includes Def Jam Records and Phat Farm is the dynamic Russell Simmons. His multimedia empire comprises Rush Communications, Def Jam Records, and Def Pictures (Simmons coproduced *The Nutty Professor*). He has worked with many top hip-hop groups and performers, including Run DMC, Foxy Brown, Jay-Z, and LL Cool J. In addition, he has created an impressive apparel empire. In 1992 he launched the Phat Farm clothing line; the secondary label Baby Phat followed in 1999. These companies produce approximately $150 million in annual sales—especially impressive considering that no mainstream department store would initially touch Phat Farm.

The influence of the street on runway couture—fashion in the mid-1980s meant Chanel models bedecked with gold chains and hip-hop-inspired, over-the-top accessories—propelled Simmons into fashion. Equally astute in spotting fashion and music trends, he noted that the style evolved from many artists represented by his companies: "Hip-hop is a strong branding community. People in the community move as an army." The hip-hop phenomenon was not lost on mainstream Seventh Avenue designers such as Tommy Hilfiger and Ralph Lauren.

The Phat Farm and Baby Phat customers, explains Simmons, "are coming from a culture that is very brand-conscious. These people come from places where they don't have a lot but they want everything that is special. They are the trendsetters. It's always the underclass that creates style attitude in America. A trend that's from the underclass can happen overnight and reach Main Street." The Phat labels are not just

a wholesale brand and a retail store in Soho—they are a cultural ethos. "It's whatever your aspiration is, what you want to be perceived as," Simmons expounds. "People are concerned about their personal image and position in the world and how their look affects these aspects of themselves."

According to Simmons, the branded sportswear revolution has exploded. For instance, the debuts of Fubu, Mecca, and Phat Farm had no effect on sales of Tommy Hilfiger; there is little competition among such brands. "There is an attempt to exploit the urban audience in negative ways with cheaper fabrics and ideas, and less aspirational products," says Simmons. He emphasizes that it is people like himself who offer clothes that capture the authentic feeling of hip-hop.

Street Style Entrepreneur # Russell Simmons

"A trend that's from the underclass can happen overnight and reach Main Street."

"An asset, you don't throw away. You just have to present it in a different way."

An experienced lieutenant in Bernard Arnault's LVMH empire, Jean-Marc Loubier has overseen a stunning, decade-long transformation of Louis Vuitton and is now in the process of remaking Celine. Once best known for its ubiquitous monogram and fleur-de-lis and its patrician roots as a traditional steamer trunk supplier, Vuitton is now a thoroughly modern status brand. Loubier recalls, "When I joined the company, the opinion leaders thought it was sleeping on the styles. It was all the same products." Despite a solid balance sheet (growing from $20 million in 1960 to $900 million in 1990), Loubier sensed that "there was a crisis looming, an urgent need to reposition the brand. Everything was monogram, monogram, monogram."

Loubier was told by fashion critics and insiders, "You should stop the monogram; it's passé, it's finished."

Still, the emblem has a quasi-historical status. "We decided that it's an asset," he recalls, "and an asset, you don't throw away. You just have to present it in a different way." What Loubier then did with Louis Vuitton's image is the stuff of marketing legend: he used the company's venerable history to turn what looked trite into cutting-edge fashion and simultaneously developed innovative new products.

As part of a huge celebration of the monogram's centennial in 1996, Loubier commissioned several iconoclastic designers—Azzedine Alaïa, Vivienne Westwood, Helmut Lang—to create novel products with the signature LV monogram. Suddenly, it seemed, Vuitton was the most fashionable new accessory. "But this didn't take place in one day," Loubier notes. "It was two years of hidden work from all departments of the company, from product design to retail stores." The climax of the marketing turnaround was the hiring of Marc Jacobs as the company's designer and the launch of its first ever ready-to-wear collection. The austere first collection of precious fashion *objets*—shoes, scarves, raincoats—created a global hunger for everything Vuitton. Loubier has begun to replicate some of this marketing strategy at the long dormant label Celine, notably with the appointment of Michael Kors as designer. This latest Loubier-led evolution is already taming some of fashion's toughest critics.

Brand Builder for Famous Names

Jean-Marc Loubier

Roberto Jorio Fili

The position Roberto Fili assumed in September 1999—head of Italy's largest clothing manufacturer, Gruppo Finanzario Tessile—makes him a key player on the world fashion scene. The company, the long-time licensee of the Giorgio Armani label, is a subdivision of the huge European communications conglomerate HdP (Holding di Partecipazioni Industriali), which owns Rizzoli Corriere della Sera, fashion lifestyle magazines such as Italian *Elle,* and partial stakes in Internet ventures such as LuxLook, a high-end accessories site.

Prior to his debut at GFT, Fili reigned as president of Calvin Klein Europe. "Now the fashion world is a small global village," says Fili. He helped Klein understand that he needed European partners in order to be competitive both price-wise and fit-wise. "I'm a tall man, but when I wear a shirt made in the United States, the sleeves are too long," says Fili. "In Europe, our clients must be fit exactly."

During his tenure at Calvin Klein, Fili analyzed the emerging predominance of American sportswear, which has taken center stage from French and Italian couturiers such as Christian Lacroix and Giorgio Armani. He notes, "America often stays ahead of Europe not necessarily in terms of fashion but in the way it interprets lifestyle. American designers such as Ralph Lauren are more pragmatic and more free."

Fili was courted assiduously by Milan's GFT, and the position entails continuing contact with the burgeoning global fashion economy as well as more effective use of his business background. It is also a return: Fili worked at GFT in the early years of his career, starting as an assistant area sales export manager. "At the time, GFT was not an international company, and it was just starting to move from the mass market to the designer, signing with Armani and Valentino," he recalls. He built his luxury brands season after season, creating and exploiting the 1980s hunger for designer Italian goods. His most important marketing and development strategy goals are creating

value for GFT's brands; entering into long-term licensing agreements with international brands; and creating joint ventures, mergers, and alliances to build GFT's consumer base.

"Today there is a completely new type of consumer," states Fili. These consumers have the aspiration but not the means to afford luxury. He contrasts this group to "the consumers at the top of the pyramid"; he plans to "transfer our expertise to design and create other products that have the same sensation of quality but at a lower price." Such new initiatives will only increase the already impressive market share of Fili and GFT.

"America often stays ahead of Europe not necessarily in terms of fashion but in the way it interprets lifestyle."

Yves Carcelle

The chairman of the dozens of fashion labels acquired by LVMH, Yves Carcelle carefully uses leather goods as the leading edge of each brand, thus maximizing the impact of the individual couture houses. At Dior, for example, the Lady Di handbag, with dangling initials and idiomatic "caned" quilt, played a key role in the revitalization of the brand and its vastly more expensive couture dresses.

In a different type of brand stewardship, Carcelle played an important role in developing the flagship Dior boutique in the new LVMH headquarters on Fifty-seventh Street. "It is fantastic to be here on this street,

which represents the best of international fashion," he says. The radically designed, light and airy store—featuring Louis XVI bergère chairs and oversized gilt-framed mirrors and complete with a unique color-changing "magic cube"—represents a twenty-first-century vision of fashion retail. Carcelle speaks of the boutique as "articulating a dream."

Carcelle circumnavigates the globe to oversee refinements to each of LVMH's brands. His micro-management has billion-dollar ramifications, although few precedents exist for valuing a designer's name on a balance sheet. Yet Carcelle understands and articulates the fragile and complex web of intangibles that constitute a logo and therefore its value. He points unerringly to a brand's individual history, its identifiable symbols, its press-worthiness—all the components of

brand authority and global recognition. Each of the dozens of luxury names he manages is unique, he says, "because a large part of the brand content is its special value for the buyer. That value comes from a sense of exclusivity, and the challenge is to retain that sense of exclusivity while deploying the brand."

> "A large part of the brand content is its special value for the buyer."

LOUIS VUITTON

The Cyberpioneers: Navigating the Electronic Frontier

Due to the highly sensory nature of fashion, Seventh Avenue was initially resistant to the lure of e-commerce. Since Tom Ford's legendary address at *WWD's* CEO summit, the fashion elite has tended to denigrate the role of technology, positing that consumers seek above all the heady experience of shopping in person. By 1999, however, the big names in fashion—especially in the luxury arena—competed to launch web sites in time for the millennium. Some turn to Wall Street's Robert Lessin, a vital liaison between investment funds and Internet businesses. Tiffany Dubin exploits another aspect of the new technology—on-line auctions—to develop the universe of fashion collectors she discovered while working at Sotheby's. This vanguard proves that Internet ventures with unique markets and products will continue to be part of fashion merchandising.

Dealmaker
for e-Fashion on
Wall Street

Robert
Lessin

Early fashion entrants into the on-line world—the Gap, L. L. Bean, J. Crew—designed content-driven sites intended to entice customers into brick-and-mortar stores. More recently, LVMH has launched and acquired numerous e-commerce sites, and traditional retailers like Neiman Marcus, Saks, and the Federated Department Stores family have been advised to enter the fray. Wall Street wizard Robert Lessin,

SoundView Corp., trades securities over the Internet and raises investment capital on line.

"The Internet provides an opportunity to form a direct relationship, a no-cost relationship, with the consumer," says Lessin, who began his career at Morgan Stanley and became its youngest-ever partner in 1987. He estimates typical dot-com start-up costs at more than $200

to lure the customer into what for many is still the alien world of dot-com shopping. "This is going to be the biggest battle in the fashion industry—if you want to spend time in our physical space, you must also spend time in our virtual space," he says.

Once consumers are there, Lessin points out, Internet sites can go on the offensive with customized

"If you want to spend time in our physical space, you must also spend time in our virtual space."

who is credited with connecting the investment-banking world with the online world, was one of the first businesspeople to see fashion in the glow of millions of web-ready computer screens. His firm, Wit

million, but, he notes, "It's not very expensive for existing brands to add dot-com to the end of the brand. Brands have legitimacy." Lessin has coaxed clients such as Tommy Hilfiger and Donna Karan into e-commerce. "The greatest brands are actually personalities: there is a Donna, a Tommy, a Calvin. Individuals want to form a relationship with the personality," he explains. Lessin advises his clients to leverage their brand names

products that traditional stores cannot stock profitably. The web has already created high expectations in the minds of the most active consumers. Lessin's equally high expectations indicate that fashion is just starting to understand the potential bottom line of the Internet.

Tiffany Dubin

Auctioneer of Vintage Style

The blue-chip background of curator Tiffany Dubin lends credibility to the Auction Network, a fashion e-tail site. In January 2000 Dubin bid farewell to the fashion department she had created at Sotheby's just a few years earlier. Before she came to Sotheby's in 1997, the venerable auction house had attracted neither young customers nor style-savvy clients. Dubin changed all that. At the "Cocktail" auction in September 1999, a sea of new collectors from the fashion-show crowd—designer-clad, eclectic, and moneyed—bid on the detritus of the cocktail culture—dresses, cocktail glasses, napkins, even the bars themselves.

Dubin had persuaded Sotheby's that creating a fashion department made good business sense. She reasoned that the passion for 1940s clothing was no less than that for Impressionism. "People didn't like the idea of a fashion department at Sotheby's—they wanted to call it 'couture,'" she recalls. Dubin vowed to do away with the snobbishness that would repel youthful customers; instead, she relied on a crop of young, fashion-savvy volunteers to keep her department afloat.

She leveraged the esteemed Sotheby's name for unprecedented marketing synergies. "Most of my job was marketing. We did 'Cocktail' because I figured I could get a liquor sponsor. My plan was to raise sponsorship to get the department self-supporting," Dubin explains. "When we thought up a concept, I'd find joint-venture partners and cobrand the sale with them. This was not selling porcelain—it wasn't like you could show a photo of a Meissen plate and wait for collectors to react." Each fashion auction Dubin masterminded had to create a stir and capture an unestablished market. "The concept started out to celebrate the art of haute couture. But that doesn't mean the same thing anymore," she declares. Dubin sensed that bidders were excited by the look of the moment rather than the tailoring history of the label; she discovered that her audience was a market of wearers rather than collectors. Dubin also capitalized on the social consciousness of the young crowd, orchestrating many of her auctions to benefit specific charities; "To Have and to Hold," Sotheby's 1998 handbag auction, raised money for a breast-cancer charity.

For her new job in the digital world, Dubin is refining her successful formula. The technology of the Auction Network allows for interactive bidding, and thus her marketing and strategic skills are being honed in new ways. In addition, she cowrote the illustrated treatise *Vintage Style*, published in 2000, and in late 2001, she opened Lair, a madcap medley of her retro favorites, within Henri Bendel.

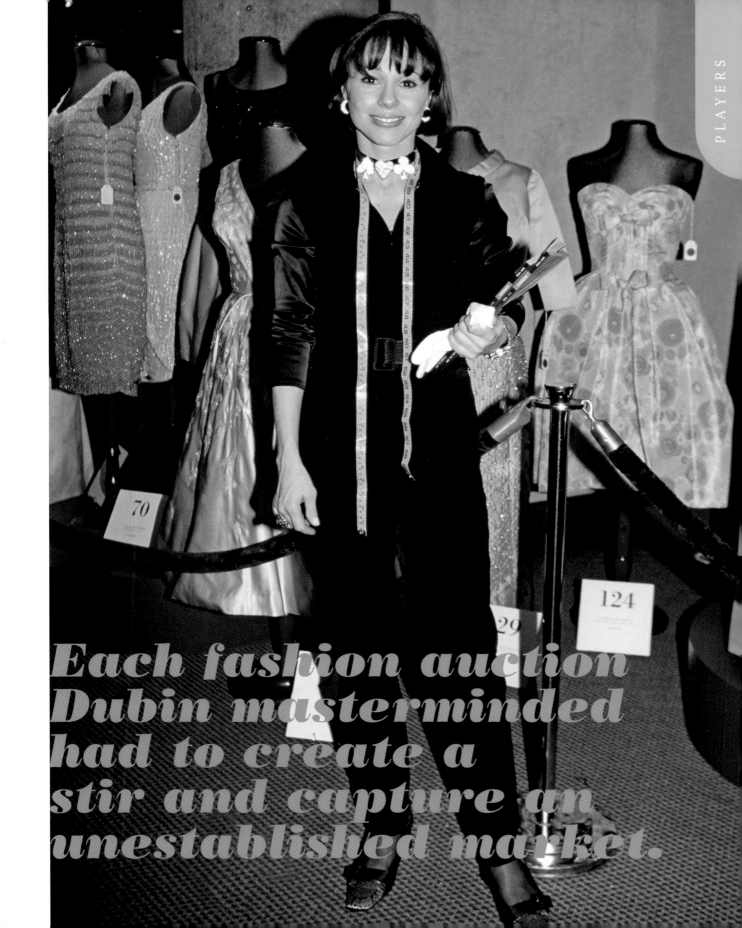

70

29

124

Each fashion auction Dubin masterminded had to create a stir and capture an unestablished market.

The Power Brokers: Negotiating the Fashion Deal

The business of fashion requires that the most serious of minds are employed in the service of the most whimsical and frivolous. These business brokers have a vast range of responsibilities. Attorneys such as Henry Welt and Peter Barack must negotiate the intangible assets of a fashion label—the value of its name, for instance—as well as the tangible ones. Recruiters line up talent for design firms new and old. Floriane de Saint Pierre, for instance, entices avant-garde designers to take positions with old-line brands, solving the question of fashion succession. Creative directors sometimes turn deal-maker: Scott Fellows of Bally, for instance, once telephoned his business-school roommate to effect a major brand buy-out. Investment bankers, such as siblings Karine and Ariel Ohana, do what it takes to sell a design firm, from sitting on corporate boards to handling the explosive personalities behind every merger and acquisition.

Karine and *Ariel*

Media Invest focused on mergers of new media, technology, and luxury long before they were popular investment arenas.

Ohana

In a European riposte to the international dominance of Wall Street investments banks, sister and brother team Karine and Ariel Ohana head Media Invest, a boutique financial house in the seventeenth arrondissement of Paris. Specialists in European mergers and acquisitions, they are widely known in Europe and elsewhere for the 1998 acquisition of avant-garde design house Hervé Leger by huge conglomerate BCBG. For LVMH, they often serve as behind-the-scenes negotiators.

The entrepreneurial siblings formed their company in 1994 along with another brother, Laurent, who is based in New York, and Manhattan real-estate tycoon Edward Milstein. Media Invest focused on mergers of new media, technology, and luxury long before they were popular investment arenas. In a short time, the partners have established relationships with many of the key players in these industries. Perfume or accessories, television or the Internet—Media Invest is set up to handle strategic mergers and acquisitions needs for companies in these areas.

Karine Ohana managed the Sanofi perfume acquisition for Chanel in 1997 and wrote a treatise on the industry, "The Luxury Goods Market: A European Outlook," which has been quoted in financial publications worldwide. She points out that there has been an economic shift—a major global consolidation—in most luxury companies, including fashion labels. Media Invest works clandestinely to bring smaller companies together with larger enterprises that have the necessary infrastructure and financial assets for fashion synergy.

The firm's strategy is working. Unlike the United States, where luxury brands remain dominated by independent designers, Europe has given birth to luxury conglomerates. Many think that the American fashion industry's stubborn independence—even isolationism—in the second half of the twentieth century has undermined the global importance of the nation's fashion luxury brands. The Ohanas are on hand to usher in a different future for Europe.

Floriane de Saint

Fashion recruiter Floriane de Saint Pierre is the industry's chic seeker of high-fashion creative talent; her global headhunting efforts have changed the fashion world. She is the siren who lured designer Narciso Rodriguez from Calvin Klein to Cerruti and, also for Cerruti, poached Peter Speliopoulos from Donna Karan. "We're making a personality and soul match," states de Saint Pierre. "It's a matter of vision. People like Ralph Lauren and Jil Sander are not merely designers— they're visionaries."

Her eponymous firm is based in Paris on the old-world Faubourg St. Honoré, better known as the street of Hermès and similar luxe labels. Three-quarters of her firm's work is executive placement on the business side: jobs ranging from CFO to English-speaking salesperson. In addition, she helps clients make changes in their companies. She urged Lanvin to hire Christina Ortiz as design director for women's ready-to-wear; she also recruited Burberry's new design director, Christopher Bailey. With impressive coups like these, de Saint Pierre has become a media magnet.

Her early job training was gained between 1984 and 1990 in the finance department of Christian Dior. She saw firsthand the results of Bernard Arnault's emphasis on building what she calls "a coherent in-house creative team moving away from licensing to direct control of the brand." De Saint Pierre goes to every major couture show and carefully follows the fashion industry in the United States and Europe. Every month or two, she travels to New York for weekend-long scouting expeditions: "We keep our eyes wide open."

In the wake of Tom Ford's triumphal revamp of Gucci, an American designer has become the symbol of a forward-thinking label, young or old. Similarly, de Saint Pierre has opened up the exclusive club of French couturiers to Americans, and with American designers at the helm of venerable French houses such as Celine and Louis Vuitton, the design world feels smaller. "It's more tribalism than globalism," she declares. "They have to have the same kind of person at every level, exuding the brand. It's not about age or nationality; it's about having the same fundamental point of view."

Headhunter
for Biggest
Fashion Houses

Pierre

"We're making a personality and soul match. It's a matter of vision."

Henry

With his cigar, Fifty-seventh Street corner office, and modern art collection, erstwhile intellectual-property lawyer Henry Welt now acts as business consultant for an array of fashion brands. After graduating from Columbia University Law School, he started a law firm geared to family businesses. In 1990, seeking broader services for his clients, he joined the midsize Manhattan law firm Kronish Lieb Weiner Hellman, establishing the first family business practice group within a law firm. In June 2000, Welt left to start his own consulting firm with clients like award-winning Perry Ellis and menswear designer Sandy Dalal.

"It was the beginning of the huge transfer of wealth to postwar baby-boomers," Welt recalls. In family-controlled companies, the transfer of power between generations is fraught with difficulties. Decisions about, for instance, overseas manufacturing versus domestic plants take on a new importance. "In a family business, the family member who is in charge of running the factory will feel threatened by family members proposing to go offshore," he says.

Attorneys for family businesses must take into account the egos and financial interests of family members who are sometimes at odds. Welt comments, "If a person who is in business with his family calls up his lawyer and says, 'I have a corporate deadlock—what is the applicable New York law?,' he's asking a very different question from someone from a public company or from a private company that's not family-dominated." Indeed, Welt has focused on what he calls the "non-business, nonlegal" side of transactions. He brings in psychiatrists and family therapists to address the issues that arise from any family business, whatever the size or product.

Even while a partner at Kronish Lieb, Welt on occasion took on executive roles in various luxury companies. For several years, he was CEO of renowned jewelry company Van Cleef & Arpels, and from 1995 to 2000 he acted as chairman of the board for the Paloma Picasso accessories-design company. About his unusual multifaceted role, Welt comments, "I love having as clients companies in which personalities dominate the business."

With his own consulting company, Welt better accommodates his clients' evolving needs. He has become more involved in intellectual property, which includes licensing and e-business. "In this logo-driven era, it is the off-balance-sheet items that are the most fundamental," Welt maintains. "If you take the Chanel logo away from Chanel, what does the company have left?"

Welt

"In this logo-driven era, it is the off-balance-sheet items that are the most fundamental."

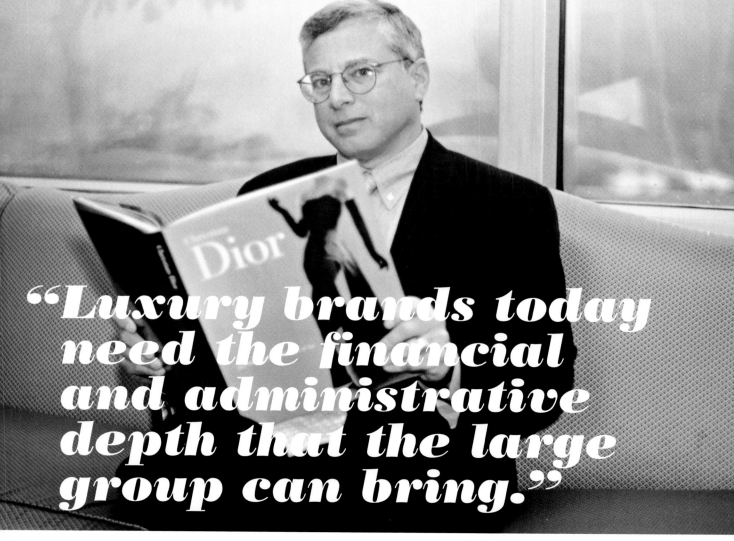

Peter Barack

"Luxury brands today need the financial and administrative depth that the large group can bring."

LVMH does not lack for in-house attorneys, either in Paris or in New York. Nonetheless, it is Peter Barack and the sixty-lawyer firm he has built in Chicago, Barack, Ferrazzano, Kirschbaum, Perlman & Nagelberg, that has handled many LVMH transactions. Wealthy international families and companies such as Wagonlit Travel and Salomon Ski also use Barack's firm, far removed though it is from fashion's center of gravity, to negotiate huge transactions that affect the face of the industry globally. In addition, the firm serves numerous telecommunications and banking companies.

Years ago, a chance encounter with LVMH's chairman, Bernard Arnault, gave the Chicago native his toehold in international fashion deal-making. Barack recalls, "I met Bernard in his hometown of Rubaix, just north of Paris, when he was a young real-estate developer." Arnault's family was in the construction development business, specializing in resort condominiums; the young men's friendship led Barack in 1977 to negotiate Arnault's first foray into investing in America, a $20-million deal to build a large condominium complex near Palm Springs, Florida.

Two decades later, Barack executed his biggest deal ever for his friend— LVMH's $3-billion purchase of DFS, Duty-Free Shoppers, a strategic worldwide outlet for all LVMH brand merchandise. "Bernard is rigorous in his thinking, like a mathematician. And decisive. Coming out of real estate, he has a great sense of cash flow," says Barack. "He brought to fashion an appreciation of larger business complexities and the opportunities inherent in deploying strategies across a conglomerate." Barack is equally astute and determined.

Barack has also shepherded some smaller LVMH acquisitions, such as cosmetics companies Urban Decay, Hard Candy, and BeneFit. These seemingly small acquisitions are part of a complex maneuver: such companies, like the fashion houses, provide fashion merchandise and beauty products for Sephora, LVMH's international chain of beauty emporiums. Sephora, like DFS, provides a controlled mass distribution system for elite brands.

Making deals has been Barack's passion, and his experience has given him unusually broad insight into emerging fashion business trends. He notes, "Obviously there is a lot of consolidation in the beauty and fashion industries. Luxury brands today need the financial and administrative depth that the large group can bring, as long as the group allows the creative people the freedom to be themselves and do what they do best." Barack believes that the trend toward consolidation will insure the future of the world's most rarefied brands, supporting creative assets with financial ones.

Scott Fellows has a well-defined charge as creative director of the luxury leather-goods brand Bally: he must reposition the sleepy, 150-year-old Swiss label in the universe of contemporary fashion. Before joining Bally, Fellows led a determined but ultimately fruitless attempt to steer family-owned Ferragamo onto the Italian fashion superhighway paved by Gucci, Prada, and Fendi. "We were trying to drive them to a point of view and make them stand behind it," he says. "We did remarkable things in gaining consistency in the brand and with shops in shops." After Ferragamo, Fellows and his team of marketing executives and design-savvy merchants flirted with acquiring brands like Saint-Laurent and Pucci. Fellows decided on Bally, which was owned by a holding company and gushing red ink.

With a business degree from Harvard, Fellows is as comfortable with leveraged buyouts and global distribution systems as with luxury products. With buyout firm Texas Pacific Group, owner of such diverse companies as J. Crew, Ducati Motors, Del Monte Foods, and Oxford Health Plans, Fellows aims to parlay the undervalued business into a global player. He says, "Everybody had looked at Bally—from Louis Vuitton to Gucci—but to turn it around was problematic because of the diluted earnings and drop in stockholder value." Even the multibillion-dollar TPG was not eager to buy Bally, but Fellows persuaded TPG managing director (and business-school roommate) Abel Halpern that the company could be turned around and run profitably or resold.

Since 1999, Fellows has radically refocused the company's strategy, moving the corporate headquarters from Zurich to just outside Milan and downsizing the retail network by about half. Yet the cutbacks also herald the debut of a new boutique look for Bally: in April 2001, Fellows inaugurated a hip new prototype, designed by Australian architect Craig Bassam, in Berlin. The finely crafted, minimalist shop—a two-story oak box with dovetailed columns, red lacquer shoebox displays, and walnut stools—will be followed by shops in Los Angeles and elsewhere.

Fellows is determined to return Bally to its alpine-style roots and the image of Switzerland as the playground of the jet set. "French and Italian products have their individual national styles," he says. "We will combine traditional Swiss precision and old-world craftsmanship with modern shapes and designs." If Fellows's metamorphosis is successful, he may change not only the image of Bally but also the Swiss perception of corporate America and its consumers.

Repositioner of Global Brand **Scott**

Timothy Greenfield-Sanders

"We will combine traditional Swiss precision and old-world craftsmanship with modern shapes and designs."

Fellows

Illustration Credits

Arnaldo Anaya-Lucca: 83
Sonia Arakawa: 20 (with graphics by
Nadine Cene and Virtual Design Studio)
Fernando Bengoeclea: 80
Daniel Benningus: 66
Marco Bertoli: 142
Britt Bivens: 24–25
Andrew Boyd: 121
Gary Brotmeyer: 43
Anna Clopet: 56, 171, 177, 182, 196, 199
James Patrick Cooper: 100
Deborah Cox: 106, 107
Harold Daniels: 36–37, 121
Patrick DeMarchelier: 48
Sante d'Orazio: 85
Stephen Gan: 49
Oberto Gili: 85
Tria Giovan: 151
Cati Gonzalez: 161, 163, 181
Timothy Greenfield-Sanders: 9, 17, 92,
179, 205
Mary Hilliard: 134, 135, 193
Hassan Jarane: 133, 158
Jean François Jaussaud: 16
James Kaliardos: 62–63
Jim Kamp: 202
Carey Adina Karmel: 34
Bill King: 116
Nikolas Koenig: 126
Ziv Koren: 162
Karen Kuehn: 76
David La Chapelle: 54–55
Karl Lagerfeld: 46
Peter Langway: 38

Annie Leibovitz: 48
Dah Len: 129, 130, 131
Jennifer Livingston: 86
Stephen McBride: 181
Patrick McMullan: 113, 125, 172
Sheryl Nields: 97, 98–99
Andrea Ott: 30
Van Peel: 153
Gianni Pezzani: 143
Arianne Phillips: 102
Librado Romero: 144
Eurydice Sanchez: 22
Michele Silver: 201
Carter Smith: 94, 95
Philip Smith: 152
SocioX: 44–45 (with photographs and
digital retouching by Nadine Cino &
Chao Yang Yan, vir2Ldesign studio)
Gerardo Somoza: 88, 89, 136–37, 154,
157, 190
Studio Edelkoort: 18, 19
Cleo Sullivan and Matthew Rolston: 96
Jurgen Teller: 86
Stacis Timonere: 121
Robert Trachtenberg: 79
Ike Ude: 69
Kenneth Willardt: 140
Firooz Zahedi: 84

Thanks to *aRude*, *Chicago Sun Times*, Laura Daniels, East Meets West, Edelkoort Inc.,
InStyle, Annie Leibovitz, *License!*, Pantone, *Paper*, Promostyl, *New York Times*,
New York Times Magazine/Fashions of the Times, Saks Incorporated, Tatoo Photography,
Taxi, *Vibe*, *Visionaire*, and Amy Wesson for permission to reproduce illustrations.